"THE ADVANTAGES OF WELL DESIGNED URBANIZATION Al ___ ___ ___ THEY CAN CONTRIBUTE TO T... SOLUTIONS TO MANY OF THE PROBLEMS THE WORLD IS FACING TODAY, INCLUDING INTEGRATION OF MIGRANTS"

Dr. Joan Clos,
Under-Secretary-General and Executive Director, United Nations Human Settlements Programme (UN-Habitat) and Secretary-General of the Habitat III Conference

CONTENTS

ACKNOWLEDGMENTS

We are grateful to H.E. Dr. Talal Abu-Ghazaleh for his vision, and support throughout the process of preparing this event and publishing the book. Mr. S. Khan's deep understanding of the role of partnership and cooperation in achieving goals guided us through this journey.

We are honored by the presence and the remarks of the distinguished dignitaries and excellencies at the 18 May 2016 event and we would like to express our deep appreciation to all session chairs, moderators, and speakers for their invaluable contributions to the event and the book.

We are grateful to Dr. Joan Clos, Executive Director of UN Habitat and the Secretary General of the Habitat III Conference and Yamina Djacta, Director of UN Habitat, New York Office, for their support in the migration initiative.

UCLG was very supportive of this effort and made it possible by contributing the time and energy of local authorities and officials. We also want to acknowledge the indisputable assistance and cooperation offered by all our esteemed co-organizers.

We thank Mr. Filiep Decorte, Ms. Francesca de Ferrari, Mr. Angel Gomez, and Ms. Angela Simon, for their contribution during the preparations of the meeting. CSU fellow Antonieta Castro-Cosio and our interns Alex Spatz, Courtney Prince, Inna Branzburg, and Marilyn Cheong were very helpful at every stage.

INTRODUCTION

The meeting, which took place on 18 May 2016 at the ECOSOC Chamber at the UN headquarters, was organized by the Consortium for Sustainable Urbanization, the United Nations Human Settlements Programme (UN-Habitat), TAG, the United Nations High Commissioner for Refugees, the International Organization of Migration, the International Labour Organization, United Cities and Local Governments, the Global Migration Group, the American Institute of Architects – NY Chapter, and Network 11.

More than half of the world's refugees and displaced populations live in urban areas, often in fragile cities with high levels of inequality. If unplanned, migration and forced displacement can lead to the formation of informal settlements and worsen existing inequalities, social tensions, risks, and a lack of access to basic services and infrastructure. Despite this, there are ample examples of cities across the world that have highlighted the potential for these vulnerable populations to live a dignified life. Furthermore, these examples have demonstrated the significance of refugees and migrants in contributing to economic growth within a geographic region if properly integrated into society both socially and spatially. The new Global Alliance for Urban Crises has established the principle of how to manage migration flows and displacement as both a humanitarian and developmental challenge.

To that end, both the Sustainable Development Goal 11 on "Sustainable Cities and Communities" and the New Urban Agenda provide the opportunity to highlight the power of urban planning and design within this capacity. This event helped to shape objectives leading up to the High Level Summit on Refugees and Migrants that has been planned for 19 September 2016.

To effectively progress, migration flows must be accepted as incidents to be planned for with a focus on addressing them through capacities of design, management, innovations, technical expertise, information and communication technologies, and political will. There was an overall optimistic sentiment exuded throughout this event, expressing the belief that migration can be managed in an efficient manner and in turn, offer positive contributions to urban societies. The purpose of this book is to surmise these sentiments and to offer hope and guidelines moving forward in addressing this challenge and recognizing its associated opportunities.

Board of Directors
Consortium for Sustainable Urbanization

PREFACE

H.E. Dr. Talal Abu-Ghazaleh, Chairman of TAG Organization, Chair of CSU Honorary Council, and Co-Chair of Network 11

Mass migrations - regardless of whether the cause is war, lack of economic opportunity, or religious beliefs - result in major displacements and human suffering. The problem, therefore, is how to host large numbers of people on a temporary basis. These temporary arrangements often become permanent. Therefore, settlements must be planned to function for a very long time and be able to expand and contract during their existence. It is hoped that individuals and families will be accommodated in more permanent settlement within the larger community. Having grown up in such a settlement and survived it, I know first hand what it means to be a refugee. This is an extremely important topic for millions of people all over the world. This book will be a tribute to everyone who is displaced against his or her will.

FOREWORD

H.E. Mr. Jan Eliasson, Deputy-Secretary-General of the United Nations

I am pleased to be with you today and I thank the organizers for taking this important initiative.

On the 19th of September the General Assembly is convening a Summit on large movements of refugees and migrants.

There are many important issues to address: the causes of forced displacement; the safety of migrants and refugees as they cross international borders; and not least support for host countries to integrate newcomers into their communities.

When we deal with the challenge of integration, we must very much focus on cities. It is in cities where most migrants and refugees in the end will settle.

While it is true that many refugees, especially in Africa and the Middle East, reside in camps, many more settle and work in host communities. In fact, just one-quarter of all refugees reside in camps according to the UN High Commissioner for Refugees.

More than half the number of refugees around the world live in urban areas. In Turkey, less than 10 per cent of the more than 2.5 million Syrian refugees reside in camps. In Jordan, around 20 per cent of registered Syrian refugees live in camps. In Lebanon, there are no camps –except for Palestinians- and over one million registered refugees live across communities in all over the country.

While most of the humanitarian assistance goes to refugees living in camps, the "urban refugees" –if you allow that expression- are largely overlooked. They often end up living in slums or informal settlements on the fringes of the cities, in overcrowded neighborhoods and in areas prone to flooding, sanitation hazards and disease.

Generally, they have a hard time finding their way to camps or reception centers, which in some cases, are established for their support. And the UN system, for its part – I must admit- cannot provide services in the same way as we can in camps.

With this in mind, UNHCR in 2009 changed its policy and practice towards refugees in cities and towns. It is now working closely with national authorities, municipalities and local communities and authorities to protect urban refugees, respecting of their refugee status.

There is much for us to do. Every day, millions of refugee children are unable attend school. Every day, the dignity and well-being of millions of people is compromised due to lack of basic services and job opportunities.

The report of the Secretary-General, prepared for the 19 September Summit draws attention to the important role of local authorities. They, many of you here today, are at the forefront in providing refugees access to housing, education, healthcare and employment.

We should bear in mind that refugees and IDPs often are just a small proportion of those who are swelling the ranks of cities, while the speed of urbanization is getting faster.

But the Secretary-General's report notes that rural poverty, natural disasters and environmental degradation are very much contributing to the numbers of persons moving to cities today.

The frequency and intensity of these factors are expected to rise, not least as a result of climate change. Urban planners need to take these movements and trends into account.

Let us also remember that, even if cities struggle to accommodate large flows of migrants, they also largely benefit from their presence and work.

As Bill Swing, Director-General of the International Organization for Migration, has said: "Migrants need cities – and cities need migrants".

In many countries in the world, immigrants often take up low-paying jobs and provide services in areas like domestic work, agricultural labour, and home-care.

Let us also recall that in major cities around the world, neighborhoods that were once in decline are being revitalized thanks to the presence and hard work of immigrant groups.

New businesses are established both by and for migrant communities, creating new jobs and contributing to the tax base. Diaspora groups are developing new trade partners as the demand for goods from their home countries rises.

The links between diversity and opportunity are nowhere as clear as in today's cities. The two-way dynamics between migration and cities is increasingly being recognized as a positive factor.

Let me again in closing refer to the Secretary-General report and draw your attention to a challenge mentioned there that seems to get more serious by the day.

That is the very real problem of growing xenophobia, and intolerance, polarization and discrimination.

As migrants and refugees continue to arrive ? and there are no signs that these flows will diminish any time soon ? we must resolve to uphold and implement the principle of every human being's equal value. This is a fundamental human right, never to be compromised.

There is particular reason to be concerned about political rhetoric that stigmatizes refugees and migrants. We must do everything possible to counter this false and negative narrative. We must dispel the myths about migrants and migration which tend to poison the public discourse.

Let us build our policies on the realization of the value that migrants bring to our societies: economic and demographic growth, development, not least through remittances, and I want to add: the beauty of diversity in our nation states.

Let us ensure that the public has access to accurate and unbiased information. For this reason, the Secretary-General is proposing a global campaign against xenophobia. I very much hope that cities and city leaders will take up this challenge.

In closing, let me thank you once again for bringing this great community of city planners together here in New York. As we work towards the Summit on September 19 and to Habitat III in Quito in October, I look forward to learning more about your initiatives and commitments locally, nationally and internationally.

PERSPECTIVE FROM THE UN-HABITAT

Dr. Joan Clos, Under-Secretary-General and Executive Director, United Nations Human Settlements Programme (UN-Habitat) and Secretary-General of the Habitat III Conference

The world's attention has turned to age-old phenomena: people on the move, on the run for conflict, displaced by natural hazards, or just seeking better opportunities.

Its scale, speed and international dimension are however unprecedented since World War II. There are one billion persons considered migrants worldwide, of whom approximately one quarter have crossed international borders, with the majority moving from city to city. It is perceived as a deepening and increasingly humanitarian crisis. We strongly believe that this should not only be seen as a humanitarian challenge but also a development challenge and opportunity.

This is in essence how cities have taken shape over time, merging people and cultures to shape new identities. With more people on the move than ever before, migration is an irreversible trend that will continue to be an integral part of sustainable urban development.

We see that local authorities struggle to support the needs of migrants. Housing in urban areas remains a significant challenge. Cities also face difficulties providing adequate basic services for refugees and migrants, while host communities in many cases feel pressured out of both the housing and job market. This is a difficult balance for local authorities.

However, if well managed, an influx of refugees and migrants can be an opportunity for revival, growth and innovation in cities. The role of local authorities is critical in this regard. Good policies, developed with local authorities, can help shape inclusive urban development. Using local knowledge and capacities can identify and implement solutions that are longer lasting, building bridges between humanitarian response and sustainable urban development to prevent millions of people from being further diminished on the margins of cities without access to basic needs, livelihoods and income opportunities.

These are all issues of concern to UN-Habitat. Based on our experience with urban planning and design, urban legislation and economic development, we have developed several intiatives that address issues arising from urban migration.

SDG 11 calls for more participatory, integrated and sustainable human settlement planning and management in all countries, something which should be used to include both refugees and migrants in longer term urban development plans.

In several cities in Somalia and Iraq, new approaches to accommodate and integrate temporary and protracted displacement as part of planned city extensions are starting to bear fruit. It enables improved access to jobs and basic services and social inclusion of displaced within the wider urban community while ensuring that investments made to deal with a crisis are contributing to longer term sustainable urbanisation.

In Jordan, we are working with local actors to finance and build affordable housing to increase housing supply, while at the same time continuing to look for solutions that can support local authorities to cope with the large influx of refugees and migrants at the urban level.

Migration needs to be accounted for when planning for urban sustainable development. The World Humanitarian Summit next week offers an opportunity in this regard, especially through the Global Alliance for Urban Crises which is building new partnerships between local government networks, humanitarian and development actors, and urban professionals to promote new and more effective ways of tackling the challenges that surface in urban areas. These are issues we as UN-Habitat also will bring forward into Habitat III to take place in Quito in October this year, making sure the New Urban Agenda brings onboard local actors to find opportunities and solutions that meet the requirements of today's refugees and migration trends.

Please see the video message below from the Conference on Migration, Refugees and Cities organized by the City of Firenze, in 2015.

https://www.youtube.com/watch?v=z3W6Ob9qcAY&feature=youtu.be

PERSPECTIVES FROM THE UNITED NATIONS

General Assembly (GA)

H.E. Mr. Michel Tommo Monthe, Acting President, United Nations General Assembly, Representative of Cameroon to United Nations

Having a discussion on Migrants and Refugees in Cities is both extremely timely and extremely necessary. It is timely because during the Humanitarian Summit in Istanbul (May 2016), New York in September919 September 2016, Migration summit), and Quito in October (Habitat3), member-states have an opportunity to put some meat on the bones of the commitment they made in the 2030 Agenda, to bring about more inclusive and sustainable cities and urban areas and to ensure safe, orderly, regular migration are full of respect for the human rights of migrants, refugees, and displaced persons. This discussion is also necessary because at this very moment, the international community is struggling, both to come to terms with the challenges and opportunities posed by the rapid rate of urbanization and to respond humanely, adequately, to an incredible, global, humanitarian refugee crisis.

The relationship between these two challenges is becoming increasingly clear. Many of the world's 60 million displaced persons and an estimated 244 million international migrants and refugees live in urban state areas. Displaced people in particular, generally live in sub-standard housing and in informal settlements and do not receive the assistance required to support immediate needs and find longer-term solutions for their plight. There is occurring at the time, when the proportion of the world's population living in urban areas is rapidly increasing and expecting to add some 2.5 billion people to the urban population by 2050. How we respond to this trend will, in some respect, go a long way to the demanding, whether we live up to the ambition of the SDGs, the Addis Ababa Agenda, and the Paris agreement.

Both migration and urbanization have the potential to usher in the new era of new well being, transformation, resource efficiency, and economic growth. Throughout history, civilization has consistently relied on migration to drive economic development and in recent times, we have seen many developing countries, particularly in the Asia-Pacific and African regions, benefit greatly from urbanization. Of course, large-scale movement of refugees and migrants together with rapid urbanization will also pose challenges. Poverty for example, is often heavily concentrated in urban areas. Nearly 1 billion city-dwellers still live in slums. Inequalities are more profound in urban areas and hosting communities face enormous pressure on and competition for, scarce social services, accommodation, and jobs, often resulting in dangerous social tensions.

As we look forward, the World Humanitarian Summit, the High Level Meeting on Migrants and Refugees, and Habitat III, therefore, we have to realize that the business-as-usual approach will simply not in any way fit for our purpose. We must be mindful of the big picture of today's population dynamics and benefits of migration. We must work towards more strategic long-term solutions including to more predictable financing, a more equitable burden-sharing. Above all, we must do all we can to live up to our shared commitments to leave no one behind but advancing international solidarity and protecting the rights of the most vulnerable."

Economic and Social Council (ECOSOC)

H.E. Mr. Sven Jurgenson, Vice-President of ECOSOC and Permanent Representative of Estonia to the United Nations

It is my pleasure to address this discussion on meeting critical challenges on migration in cities on behalf of the President of the Economic and Social Council, His Excellency Mr. Oh Joon, permanent representative of the Republic of Korea to the United

Nations.

The topic of this discussion, which considers two significant global trends of the 21st century: the increasing mobility of populations, both within countries and across international borders, and the growing number and share of people residing in cities. Both phenomena are recognized in the 2030 Agenda For Sustainable Development. Migration features prominently in several SDG targets, in particular target 10.7 which seeks to facilitate orderly, safe, regular, and responsible migration and mobility of people, including through the implementation of planned and well-managed migration policies. SDG 11, in turn, aims to make cities inclusive, safe, resilient, and sustainable. The topic of today's meeting, meeting critical challenges in migration in cities, reminds us of the importance of integrating migration policies with urban development policies and planning.

Recognizing the crucial role of cities in efforts to achieve sustainable development, the ECOSOC in 2014 devoted its first ever integration segment to the topic of sustainable urbanization. The segment provided a multi-stakeholder platform to demonstrate how urbanization can serve as a catalyst for sustainable development.

The world's cities are growing both in size and in number. In 2016, 4 billion people, nearly 55% of the world's population, lived in urban settlements. United Nations projections indicate that by 2030, urban areas will be home to 60% of the world's population. Almost all of the growth in the urban population of the world will occur in the cities and towns of developing countries. Governments must be proactive in planning for future urban growth if they are to reap the benefits that cities offer by virtue of their size and density of population. They must also minimize the adverse environmental impacts urbanization. Policies and programs are needed to develop critical infrastructure and provide access to essential services, including secure access to water and sanitation, healthcare, schooling, land tenure, and adequate housing, especially for the urban poor. In addition, policies are needed to improve solid waste management systems and to increase energy efficiency in transport and housing. These are just a few examples.

Migration from rural to urban areas is one of the main contributors to the growth of cities. People are drawn to cities because of the myriad of opportunities cities offer to those in search of a better life. Cities are economic engines, as well as social and cultural political hubs. Cities offer newcomers the prospect of higher incomes, better access to education and healthcare, diversified labor markets and enhanced opportunities for cultural and political participation. Yet, despite the many advantages associated with urban life, many cities face persistent challenges in relation to poverty and inequality. Migrants can be especially vulnerable to urban poverty and social exclusion. Those who arrive in a city in search of physical and economic security are often confronted with barriers that hinder their full participation in the economic, social, cultural, and civic dimensions of city life.

Today's cities are global and cosmopolitan, largely because they were destinations of many of the world's 244 million international migrants. The 1994 Cairo Program of Action emphasized the need for international migrants to participate fully in society. This becomes possibly only by protecting their human rights, by ensuring access to education, healthcare and other essential services and by incorporating migrants into the world of work.

I look forward to discussing further challenges and opportunities posed by large movements of refugees and migrants, including the protection of their human rights, partnerships among the countries of origin, transit and destination, as well as the root causes for large movements of refugees and migrants at the high level meeting on the 19th of September. We know that migrant, refugee and Diaspora communities can bring economic dynamism and renewal to their host communities, and that they can contribute to job creation and help to reinforce the tax base. Unfortunately today, many migrants face discrimination and are the target of xenophobic rhetoric. Cities are at the forefront of welcoming newcomers. For this reason, I hope that many mayors as possible will join the global campaign to counter xenophobia, which is being launched as part of the high level event to address large movements of refugees and migrants on the 19th of September 2016.

High Level Meeting to address large movement of refugees and migrants (HLM)

H.E. Ms. Dina Kawar, Representative Jordan to the United Nations and co-facilitators for the UN General Assembly (UNGA) high-level meeting (HLM) to address large movements of refugees and migrants

We've heard a lot about the importance of immigrants, refugees and the successful urbanization in order to deal with it, but how do we do that? We all agree on the issues, we all agree that certain issues have to be tackled, but I want to talk a little bit about the issues on refugees and if I may, about my country, Jordan, which is hosting 1.3 million refugees, which is almost 20% of our population. And why I am saying that is because obviously, the issue of urbanization is one of the most complicated matters. Our cities are being over-burdened, over-loaded, and the country, being the second poorest country in water is having to struggle with sharing the little water it has with the refugee intake.

Now how do we do that? We could have sulked and cried because much of the money and help that have been promised have not arrived, we could say we could not deal with it and close our borders and say no more, we could say we can't offer schooling because we don't have enough resources, we can't offer medical, but no, this is not in our morality and not in our way of doing things, we have been the most generous and open in this aspect.

But, we have started thinking positively "how can we do?" And some of the things that we've done, apart from sharing schools and medication, we've gone one step further by saying "how do we create employment?" and that is one of the things that we have been working on. We started working it during the London Conference and we hope that this model is going to be introduced in the September 19th Conference, which is to say creating free economic zones, allowing for the Syrian refugees to work in Jordan and to be able to provide their families with an income. Why? Because the refugee according to the UN says at least 17 years and you can't expect a whole generation to stay taking income from money from the UN assistance without having to pay back. We've also started turning to the world and saying "okay, you want us to provide medication, you want us to provide schooling, you want us to provide this and that, then help us, stand on our feet."

So the question here that we need to say is that we cannot put all countries on the same level. We've been hearing that yes, we need to do A, B, C, and D, yes, refugees are…, but we have to remember one thing, a country like Jordan is not like a country that's rich. And unfortunately, and allow me to be very frank today, it's only when the refugees started coming to Europe that the issue became high up on the priority list. And I'm so sad to see that, for five years we have been struggling with refugees, Lebanon has been struggling with refugees, Turkey has been struggling. I am happy that is has become an issue that is important and that is going to be discussed on the 19th of September 2016. I'm happy that President Obama is going to be having a special conference on the 20th, but when will we learn that issues that are important in the poorer countries have to be priority because we are living in a world that is globally open. You cannot disassociate issues from the poorer countries from the Europe or the States. We're talking about refugees now because refugees are a political crisis, but in 10 years, migration that will come as a flow to Europe because everybody has found out that taking the boats and going to Europe is an easy thing, and I say "easy" not to make fun of it to facilitate the issue, but to say it's doable. So these issues have to be dealt with as a global issue and we've been talking about a responsibility sharing, we've been talking about burden-sharing, and it's not a joke and it's not a slogan. The world has to realize that if we do not help countries that are suffering with refugees in the South, this problem is going to move to the North and it will become a global issue. So I hope that in the Habitat3 conference that will be held in October 2016, the issue of urbanization will be dealt in the concept of burden sharing and responsibility-sharing.

We need to find new, out-of-the-box ways of thinking about it. We have seen in Jordan some Jordanian architects, who live in Canada or some in the United States who started figuring out cheap housing, cheap ways of helping refugees, new methods of dealing with the issues and the crisis and I think that's a forum that is very interesting. Why not have in all these conferences a box that says 'New Ideas' and allow for the people how have these ideas to come in and help the UN to have cheaper housing, cheaper and better ways of dealing with problems.

Global Migration Group (GMG)

Ms. Lakshmi Puri, Assistant Secretary-General, UN Women, Global Migration Group Chair

On behalf of the 18 member United Nations Global Migration Group comprising of entities that work together to promote the application of all relevant instruments and norms relating to migration and encourage the adoption of more coherent and comprehensive and better-coordinated approaches to international migration

The context of Habitat III is very much the framework that is provided by Agenda 2030 and SDGs. And in that context, the Global Migration Group has identified within Agenda 2030 and the

SDGs, six key targets that relate to migration. And of course, target 11.7 is core, which calls for safe, orderly, regular, and responsible migration, and then all together there are 22 other targets. So this is the SDGs context of migration and as has been mentioned, very much about human rights based, about leaving no one behind, and of course, in that context, to make sure that there is coherence between the Urban Agenda that is being pursued, the New Urban Agenda that is being evolved in the context of Habitat III, and therefore the mainstreaming of migration into Habitat III and the Urban Agenda, the New Urban Agenda as well as the connections between the 19th of September 2016 event and the outcome on large movements of refugee and migrants as well as the World Humanitarian Summit – the humanitarian agenda – so the joining up of all of these agendas and the mainstreaming of migration within that.

In the context of migration, cities, as has been mentioned are the main entry points for refugees and migrants. But let's not forget that there are also, in most cases, the points, the departure points, the countries of origin and many times, countries of transit. So cities are involved in all stages of the migration cycle and that also applies to the refugee cycle that also applies to trafficking so in all of these areas.

I also want to echo very strongly that developing countries are both the main source and destination of the most refugees and internally displaced people. So the burden on developing countries cities that are already over-stressed and growing in an unplanned manner in most cases is very high. And of course in the context of therefore, analyzing the root cause an addressing them as well as the push and pull factors that go behind migration, this needs to be addressed and taken into account and also international cooperation in the many dimensions that have been mentioned must come forward. Urban areas benefit from – this is the other aspect that we at GMGC want to bring out – the win-win migration and development, the win-win of migration of peace and security, that it can be made and it is inherently a positive force so how do we ensure that it is a positive force, how do we ensure that this is recognized? This is very much linked to what has been said about the negative narrative and the global migration group is very much ready and indeed working with the Secretary General's office and with DSG to make sure that we strongly drive this campaign that you have mentioned on a positive narrative, the win-win, the positive sum and creation of migration and development.

Cities face two predominate challenges that pertain to the physical and psychological barriers to diversity and integration, correcting urban planning and urban design that keeps people out and addressing resistance to social change in the hearts and minds of the receiving communities. So as should be welcoming to new arrivals, this is the responsibility of the local governments as was mentioned also in the Secretary General's report for the 19th September meeting. The way cities are designed is an important piece of the urban diversity puzzle and can be a major obstacle to the active inclusion of new arrivals; the effective integration of migrants and refugees in cities will be the key to achieving Goal 11 of the 2030 Agenda on making cities inclusive, safe, resilient and sustainable. The inclusion of migrants and refugees is also a cornerstone for the implementation of the New Urban Agenda to be adopted in October 2016 in Quito.

Effective disaster risk reduction, this is another dimension that we must not forget to link up with migration and New Urban Agenda, to reduce exposure of the most vulnerable, including refugees and migrants will also be a key determinant for the achievement of Goal 11 of the New Urban Agenda.

And lastly as you can imagine, the Global Migration Group this year is determined to make sure that we engender, we make sure that the gender equality and women's empowerment compact of agenda 2030 which put this at the center of all of the goals and targets, but also particularly a dedicated goal, SDG 5 on achieving gender equality and empowering all women and girls, including migrant and refugee women has to be taken into account and has to be mainstreamed into both Urban Agenda as well as the migration agenda and this is what we're seeking to do at all levels and recently concluded CSW60 has indeed made a strong plea and this is a strong message to all of you who are negotiating the draft outcome document of the Habitat III that please mainstream and prioritize gender equality and women's empowerment in all the policies relating to migration and development but including urban developing in every way at the countries of origin, transit, and destination but also international norms, now there is a big opportunity for new international norms.

This is what I really wanted to draw attention to, also in CSW there is a particular mention of women refugees and their vulnerabilities and also to the fact that host communities and host countries need to be supported in order to address issues of women refugees and their vulnerabilities. So we stand ready to support member-states in their preparation for the 19th September 2016 summit which is a significant opportunity to strengthen collective action and international cooperation to ensure safety and dignity for all men and women on the move and at the same time, we want this trinity of migration, gender equality, and the New Urban Agenda to be closely linked and looped.

International Labour Organization (ILO)

Mr. Vinícius Carvalho Pinheiro, Special Representative to the UN and Director International Labour Organization (ILO) Office for the United Nations

As you know, the search for jobs is often the major driver for migration and cities are often the major destination of migrants. So these two issues are particularly related. In the case of migrants and refugees, jobs are, I think, part of the problem but also part of the solution. But let me focus on the refugees' issues and the refugee crisis.

The global discus to address the humanitarian crisis has evolved and the international community recognizes that policies need also to help refugees to obtain jobs. So employment is in fact, part of the bridge, between humanitarian and development response. Over 17-18 million documented refugees and asylum seekers and millions of more forcibly displaced persons; only a very small minority gains access to labor markets in the foreign economy. Opportunities for these people to work in conditions of employment of the right workplace are very important. So for the most part of them, law may prohibit access, and just a few that manage to find work, they do so in the foreign economy. That means a very precarious situation: Frequently a lack of respect to fundamental principles and rights to work that can result in situations of forced labor, slave labor, and child labor.

So to address this situation, let's talk about solutions, that's what you asked, Mr. Chair, and here I would just like to point out two examples that are very interesting. One is Jordan, another one is Turkey that has provided access to labor markets to improve protection, health benefits, and labor law protection. Working directly with local enterprises, to create enabling environments that help business to expand jobs and provide dividends is definitely part of the solution. For example Turkey, in a survey to over 300 businesses, big companies and small companies, over 60% said that with some additional investments, they could expand jobs for nationals and refugees. In addition, in Jordan, through the ILO's "Better Work" program, in the garment sector, we are working very closely with employers, with trade unions, with the ministry of labor, and UNHCR in a pilot initiative that will create jobs for thousands of refugees and these jobs are not being created at the expense of jobs for nationals or for other migrant workers.

So labor market institutions, access to freedom of association on collective bargaining. These issues are also important in this process to protect workers' rights. So ILO's experience shows that those countries with well developed, coherent, and coordinated achievable market policies and systems are most effective in supporting the social integration of migrants. Strong labor market information is also fundamental and policies that protect, that provide training and apprenticeship that provide opportunities for young refugees. Just to conclude, let me say that social dialogue is fundamental, in particular to avoid xenophobia. Supporting access to labor markets and the issue of mobility is a complex challenge but it is a fundamental part of the solution, in particular in bridging the humanitarian and the developmental aspects of the response to the crisis. So, when you think about urban migrants, think about work.

United Nations High Commissioner for Refugees (UNHCR)

Ms. Ninette Kelley, Director, NY Office, UNHCR

There are more than 60 million displaced persons around the world today, with the largest number of refugees displaced in over 20 years. 86% of all refugees are located in the developing world. What's not often appreciated is that over 60% of refugees are located in non-camp settings. Traditionally, the focus has been on refugees, living in camps, but the reality, as many of you well know, is far different.

In many of the world's expanding cities, especially those in the developing world, increased displacement to urban areas exacerbates existing challenges. This includes stresses on already strained urban infrastructure and additional demand on available social services. Competition and higher demand for basic goods and services often lead to price increases as well as a larger labor pool, which, depending on the size of the population displaced to these areas, can lead to competition for jobs.

Among the other challenges in urban as opposed to camp settings is identifying who the refugees are. Because urban areas are often so big, outreach is more complex. A number of good technologies and practices have been engaged to address these challenges. These include the use of community centers and outreach refugee volunteers as places to receive refugees and also identify them in communities respectively and provide them with information on how to register and how to access essential services. Use of mobile tablets for collecting information is also a useful tool, as is the use of cell phone messaging to communicate important information to a dispersed community of refugees.

Another challenge that we face is how to ensure refugees have access to essential services, especially when those services are often inaccessible or very stretched to local populations. We try to channel service delivery as much as possible through local service providers where appropriate and support those services to manage the extra demand. In addition, in urban situations, cash based interventions can be used in very dynamic and innovative ways. In fact, assistance and service delivery through cash-based initiatives are proliferating: they can be extremely efficient delivery mechanisms, providing refugees and others who benefit from them the ability to choose how best to prioritize and meet their own needs.

The availability of resources continues to be a constant constraint to humanitarian interventions as funding appeals fall consistently short of the resources that are needed. As humanitarians, we need to expand existing partnerships, and that's why events like today are extremely important. It is not just UN agencies, international NGOs or the international community that are dedicated and experienced, but importantly local institutions, the local authorities, national civil society actors, the urban planners, as many of you are, who are vital in helping us to design our programs in ways that deliver benefits not just to the refugees but also have important dividends to local communities. And these approaches we need to make much more systematic.

Certainly, efforts like the Global Alliance and the Urban Consortium present unique and wonderful opportunities to bring the best minds together to think of how we move forward. Another opportunity will be the Summit for Refugees and Migrants of 19 September, which will aim to make the response to large movements of refugees and migrants systematic: more robust, predictable, and ensuring that responsibilities for such movements are shared among states in a much more equitable manner. The countries that are closest to refugee flows bear the disproportionate burden as we see right now.

In addition to the Secretary General's ambition for migrants and the Summit, which has been reviewed today, we hope to achieve greater state commitment on responsibility sharing for refugees, drawing on established best practices. Best practices include ensuring predictable humanitarian funding at the outset of a refugee influx, to appropriately receive refugees, determine their specific needs and support immediate, life-saving interventions. To ensure a humanitarian response that is sustainable over the longer term, the objective is to deliver services as much as possible through local service providers, and to support those service providers and the communities in which refugees live. Finally, to make responses to large-scale refugee movements more predictable and more comprehensive, there is a need to bring development actors much earlier on in the process.

This response needs to become the default response, not the exception, and must be delivered in a comprehensive manner. To avoid a piecemeal approach, our network of partnerships must be expanded and our methods of doing work need to become more systematic and sustainable over the longer term.

International Organization of Migration (IOM)

Ms. Michele Klein-Solomon, Director of the Secretariat of Migrants in Countries in Crisis International Organization for Migration

I'm representing the International Organization for Migration, the principal intergovernmental organization for migration issues made of 162 members states that present in more than 142 offices worldwide.

I'm going to offer three thoughts having listened very

carefully to so many of the speakers up until now. And the three thoughts are this, on the migration side, migration is a natural phenomenon, it's not a problem to be solve it's an issue to be managed. Migration is caused and driven by many factors, some of them force, some of them voluntary, sometimes permeate, sometimes temporary, multidimensional, it's simply a reality of the world we live in today. And we need to change the paradigm about this as so many others have said. We need to see migration as both enviable and as potentially beneficial not only for individuals but for the societies and the communities that are engaged and affected. We need to change the way that we think about and talk about these issues.

Second, the best way of doing so, the best way to addressing the large movements that are the focus of this discussion today is to facilitate safe, regular and orderly migration to really develop the policies, the tools, the management approaches at all levels that can make migration something safe, regular and orderly for individuals, that societies and communities can plan for and engage in constructively. That's the vision of the sustainable development goals target 10.7 that were adopted in this institution last September. Now is the time to make that a reality, that's means protecting the rights of individuals. It means creating adequate legal channels for migration at all skills levels. It means creating a family and educational opportunities for people to move safely overseas. To creating humanitarian admissions as the mayor to my right talked about. The important message and efforts of governments like Canada in welcoming refugees and other forced migrants. It means combating human trafficking and migrant smuggling, prosecuting the proprietors while protecting the victims. And it means reducing the negative impact both for individuals and societies of irregular migration, unplanned, large movements.

Which brings me to my third point and the most important one for our discussion here today. Partnership is the

only way to go about that. And that's means not only whole of
government but whole of society approaches. They really bring
together countries of origin transit and destination, civil society
organizations at all levels; privet sector, employers and recruiters
have an essential role to play. And critically for the discussion that
we are having here this afternoon, it means bringing in the local
and municipal authorities, who are absolutely on the front lines and
who have the capacities and the interests in making this experience
positive for the newcomers and for their societies. Cities and urban
places are where those interactions take place, there where the
opportunities are created and where these opportunities are lost if
not plan for and well managed. It's in the workplaces, it's in the
shops, in schools, local government offices where those
interactions can take place in a beneficial way if they anticipated
and planned for.

In policy terms as several of my prior speakers have talked
about, migration policies generally made at the national level. But
it's a local and municipal and city level where the implications are
felt. And it's very gratifying to see so many innovations that are
being adopted by so many cities and local officials. Local notions
of citizenship and belonging recognizing the direct interest in
making people feel welcomed, in creating platforms for their
participation so that you create that dynamism and cohesion that is
so essential for the safety and well-being of individuals and for the
dynamism of economies and cultures.

Last year IOM held a first ministerial conference on
migrants and cities, and we are very happy to partner with many of
the people in this room to make that a reality. More than 600
mayor and other representatives came and shared their direct
experiences, and the challenges, and the innovative things that they
are doing. Those kinds of platforms and partnerships like the one
today are absolutely essential for sharing good ideas and showing
the pathway forward. IOM's world migration report was dedicated
to the same subject, and I really recommend that to you to have a

look. Don't worry I'm going to finish before my three-minute warning.

My last thought is that we can turn even large movements into positive if we change the way that we think about these issues and really look to welcoming newcomers in our societies. And it's precisely at the local and municipal level where that is most possible and where we need to find the partnerships to make that a reality. The September summit that my colleague from the UNHCR just mentioned here in the UN addressing large movements, from the IOM perspective on the migration side we will be working toward the global combat on safe, regular and orderly migration. That must involve local officials; it must involve the privet sector and others. There is no way for that to be a success without the engagement of the people on the front lines. We look forward to work in partnership with you going forward.

High Level Meeting to Address Large Movements of Refugees and Migrants

Mr. Fabrizio Hochschild, Deputy to the SG's Special Advisor for the High Level Meeting to Address Large Movements of Refugees and Migrants

Addressing Large Movements of Refugees and Migrants, as a challenge, and I would like to care that I would live up to it. I may do is by underlining many of the points that have been made and say why they are so relevant and hopefully could be better addressed through an outcome of the 19 September (2016) high level meeting on addressing large movement of refugees and migrants, the first ever to happened at head of states level.

I think this book is very timely, as we too easily forget, faced with the television images of refugee camps of brave units, our colleagues on beaches and on front lines elsewhere in the refugee crisis. We too often forget that one of the most active front lines is in cities and the people leading that front line is municipal workers, mayors, and their staff.

Migrants and refugees alike seek safety and the potential for livelihoods that cities can promise. Cities where such movements are now preceding considerable stress on public services, on land recourses, on public order arrangements in the cities that are subject to such influxes. But cities are also an illustration of the tensions that characterized the current global debate on refugees and migration. They illustrate the challenges that we face in better managing, better accommodating large movements. But on the other hand, they illustrate the benefits of migration, Cities are unthinkable without migrations, cities by definition cannot become cities without migration. It not just the mayor of London who is the descendant of migrants, I think that very few inhabitants of London, a city of what, 60 million by now, who don't trace their ancestors to somewhere else.

Cities are being the corporation of the benefits of migration. And perhaps no few cities demonstrate that better than the one that hosts today. The city thrives on diversity and migration. So the hostility and xenophobia our out of place. If there was one underline message it should be, we have to deal with it. We have to manage it. that we can deal with it. But the host hostility and xenophobia is present, it's also because there is a lack of information and a lack of historical memory. I think that if we all pause to reflect two minutes on those who proceeded us, our fathers, our grandfathers, our grandmothers, just go back two or three of four generations in our own families very few of us will not discover somebody there to whom we owe our existence, or at least we owe the fact that we thrived and be in this room today to the fact that migration was possible, to the fact that seeking refuge elsewhere was possible.

So xenophobia and hostility can also be an act of tremendous hypocrisy because it something that many people, humanity has long benefited from and will long benefit from. It not just those who came before us but those who came after us who many of whom with no doubt migrant, many of our children, our children's children and sadly some may also require refugee state. So this is not a problem that affects others, this isn't about how we deal better with a population that's alien and less fortunate than ourselves, this is about how we deal better with something that is a critical part of our common humanity.

Migration and becoming a refugee is not really a problem as such. The problem arises where there is an adequate sharing of responsibility. If it weren't eight countries, as distinguish ambassador of Lebanon mentioned, looking after 50% or more of the refugee population, but if that responsibility were better distributed among the 193 member states, the crisis for host countries would be much less acute. The crisis is not really one of numbers, the crisis is one, and the Secretary-General had said this, and I think it was also quoted; the crisis is one of global solidarity. And that is precisely what the aim of 19 September, the high-level meeting is, an attempt to change. The aim is there really to see can we come up with better, with more collective responses, better joined up responses. This is not a new idea, and I would caution, I mean there is obviously a great need for new ideas but many ideas already out there. Many ideas are entering into the international normative framework that governs how the international community should deal with refugee flows. The idea of responsibility sharing is integral into 1951 refugee convention, and the problem has been less a gap of ideas, or a gap in norms, or a gap in policies, than the very uneven application of the policies that we have.

And likewise on migration, this is a phenomenon that will increase and that we need better global governance, better global understanding. And it's towards those ends that the meeting on 19 September will work and I would, the mayors with their pragmatism will be a key voice in that, and I hope very much directly and through your diplomatic representatives of your member states you will be able to arch that we really take advantage of that unique opportunity to come up with a more humane way of

dealing with the challenge and one where we live the true benefits
of global mobility.

PERSPECTIVES FROM THE LOCAL AND SUB NATIONAL GOVERNMENTS

United Cities and Local Governments

H.E. Mr. Josep Roig, Secretary General of United Cities and Local Governments

The current humanitarian crisis in the Middle East provides real facts about what is going on regarding refugee and migrant movements. UCLG members and local municipalities from Jordan, Lebanon, and Turkey are informing us about the situation. For a long time cities have been places to which displaced people migrate. While states define migration policy, it is local governments that are on the front lines, welcoming migrants into communities.

Migration is both a challenge and an opportunity. For local governments, migration may contribute to the economic development of cities and bring cultural diversity, new skills, and traditions. However, when cities are called to provide emergency reception to refugees fleeing humanitarian crises situations, immense challenges arise and often place stress on available resources.

In the long term, even under normal conditions, migrants often face social and economic exclusion. We must ensure that all residents have the opportunity to integrate themselves into the network of a city and that cities are equipped to harness the potential of all who live in them. In this way, migration can be a win-win for everyone.

One of the roles of local government networks like UCLG is to coordinate knowledge sharing between cities and migrants. This has allowed us to identify a number of policy recommendations.

The first is that migration should be treated as a crosscutting issue. All municipal departments should consider migration as an issue, among others ranging from budgeting to education to urban planning. Migration does not mean instituting new services in the city; it means making existing services accessible to all. This includes ensuring migrants have access to basic services and language education, preventing segregation through urban planning, and promoting intercultural exchange through cultural activities.

This approach, to host and encourage inclusion of migrants, requires effective coordination at the city level, with other spheres of government, and with civil society. Existing residents must feel part of the process and have the opportunity to interact with new arrivals. Of course, this requires building the capacity of local practitioners; in particular, social workers and civil servants. Cultural training should be provided to allow municipal workers to better understand the needs of migrants; peer learning between cities can be a powerful tool to build capacities. For example UCLG's City-to-City program in the Mediterranean is now helping cities to share practices on the governance of migration.

Local governments also need adequate financial and human resources, particularly when they are dealing with emergency migration. It is essential for local governments to be involved in every step of national and international migration policy from definition to implementation. The Habitat3 Conference will be another opportunity to make our voice heard on this issue. While it is promising that the New Urban Agenda is very likely to recognize the role of local governments in protecting the rights of vulnerable groups such as migrants, we need to go further. We need to ensure a framework that ensures equal participation in public life, and that there is a close coordination on migration between global, national, and local levels.

We have to recognize the importance of ensuring a strong global urban alliance to cope with humanitarian crises. The hope is that the states listen to cities, and to the concerns and priorities of local governments dealing with migration on the ground. After all, citizenship should not be thought only as a passport given by states, but also as a commitment to foster and extend security, integration, and basic rights to the city to all citizens.

Council of European Municipalities and Regions

Mr. Frederic Vallier, Secretary General of the Council of European Municipalities and Regions

I represent cities and local regional governments. One reflection I have is that very often nations/states are more selfish than municipalities. Mayors confronted directly with problems are willing, and must, solve them right away. When municipalities have refugees approaching their cities, they cannot say "okay I close my borders, go to the next city", rather they have to allow entry and provide services and shelters, and work with the civil society to find solutions that ensure security is organized for welcoming refugees. Those are the first things they have to do. But then, municipalities have to provide housing, schools, and services to make sure that the integration is properly achieved—this is something we are intently working on, at the moment, in my organization.

I invite you to connect to our website at CMR.org, where you can find a series of declarations and documents describing how we tackle theses issues with our members, which are the National Associations of Municipalities and Regions all across Europe.

PERSPECTIVES FROM NON GOVERNMENTAL ORGANIZATIONS

Consortium for Sustainable Urbanization

Dr. Aliye Pekin Çelik, President, Consortium for Sustainable Urbanization

Large Movements of Refugees are on our conscience and our TVs around the clock; everyday brings heartbreaking images and stories. The Consortium for Sustainable Urbanization is based in the United States, a country comprised of immigrants; we do not view refugees and migrants as a political problem, as a humanitarian crisis, or as populations escaping potential death. Rather, we view refugees and migrants as an issue to be dealt with, an enigma, and a problem to be solved by focusing and repairing the means and methods by which people become re-settled. Refugees and migrants need access to public spaces, education, healthcare, and employment. They need resources to affect healing from the physical and social suffering they have sustained. We suggest that innovative use of information and communication technologies—mapping, planning, and design methods—can affect solutions for countries from which refugees and migrants originate, countries they inhabit in transit, and countries they seek as more permanent destinations. Existing settlement examples prove that migrants can be an economic, social and cultural asset to destination countries, when they are met with resources, acceptance and a positive attitude.

The Consortium encourages a positive narrative about refugees and migrants. These populations, whether visitors or residents, need to be integrated into society so they may start functioning and become productive contributors as well as happy individuals. Affecting productive results from the human resources pouring into any respective city requires considerable thought, organization, planning, design, investment, and infrastructure.

We must look at developing strategies to foster successful integration of migrant populations, and to support their potential to contribute to civil society. It is possible to achieve desirable results. Our emphasis is on the role of cities and local authorities, as well as tapping into the political will of the local and national leaders to find solutions. We encourage a dialogue that both grapples with useful planning and design examples and posits strategies for the successful settlement and integration of migrants and refugees. Our objective is to bring together UN delegations with urban planners, architects, academics, and local authorities—the intention is to identify practical solutions and raise the awareness of professionals with respect to their potential to contribute and affect solutions.

American Institute of Architects

Ms. Carol Loewenson, President of AIA NY Chapter, Partner, Mitchell, Giugola Architects

AIA New York is the country's oldest and largest chapter of the American Institute of Architects. As a professional organization our New York chapter alone has more than 5500 members that include traditional and non-traditional practitioners, teachers, students, and affiliated professionals. We have 27 committees that function like think tanks on subjects ranging from urban design, to risk and reconstruction, to healthcare, and the environment. These committees work both independently and collaboratively to share best practices, and discuss the pressing issues of the day. Specialists come to our Center for Architecture to speak on a regular basis. And likewise, we go out into the city's communities and schools to engage, listen and share our knowledge and problem solving abilities.

As architects, we know that we cannot change the political and social factors that have led to mass migrations. But, as architects, we also know that we can and should step up and participate to make a difference. Architects are trained to be problem solvers. This problem solving starts by listening and understanding unique conditions. We learn about history and try to learn from the past. We learn to collaborate – to work with others – with specialized training that complements our own. This includes civil engineers, structural engineers, mechanical, electrical and plumbing engineers, landscape architects, urban planners, communications, security, and a multitude of other specialists.

So while we know that we cannot change what has already happened, we can mobilize the community of architects, and the wide range of those whose collaborate in the creation of the built environment, because the consequences of these upheavals affect everyone and are everyone's problem.

As architects we can look at organizational considerations–issues of scale, size, community and identity. We can look at practical and social issues, and develop real strategies for implementation. We can help set priorities, be aware of sensitivities, identify opportunities, and establish plans for implementation. The issues to be addressed are as broad as the range of practitioners in our field: space, security, access, housing, education, healthcare, and infrastructure. Community, governance and employment are key factors to stabilize and allow migrant communities to establish roots and heal. Again, architecture cannot solve these problems on its own but it can help create the environment to allow a stable society to thrive.

In the past, the architectural community has stepped up in the face of aggression (9/11), natural disasters, Hurricanes Sandy and Katrina, and economic failure and exodus from communities in Detroit. Our code of ethics calls for it, and our training has prepared us for just this kind of challenge.

As we consider the plight of permanent refugees, decades old refugee camps, masses of forced exoduses in the Middle East, Africa, Europe and Asia, we should be collectively focusing on how to maximize the livability and sustainability of the limited resources available to address these acute problems. Creating real homes, schools, hospitals and other facilities is an extremely important part of solving these enormous problems. Using our collective experience, including the skills of professional architects, we together can provide the homeless and the displaced with homes, safety, shelter, hope and opportunities.

International Rescue Committee

Dr. Lucy Earle, Urban Advisor, International Rescue Committee and UK's Department for International Development

Two events coming up in the next months that provide an opportunity to think about the way forward: the World Humanitarian Summit and Habitat3 .

IRC has been working on bringing together these two communities – of urbanists and humanitarians – together. It's not always easy: they speak different languages, have very different perspectives and priorities. But this engagement is becoming increasingly important.

IRC is deeply concerned about current levels of displacement, and very mindful of its urban characteristics. We are pleased to see that the forcibly displaced are mentioned numerous times in the first draft of the New Urban Agenda for HIII, but the question is – what are we going to do about this?

IRC and others have used the World Humanitarian Summit and Habitat3 to galvanise an array of different actors to start talking to each other and working together on urban crises. This includes urban displacement crises. This urban expert group is being institutionalised as the Global Alliance for Urban Crises (www.urbancrises.org) and will be launched at the WHS. It's a different type of Alliance as it brings municipal authorities and professional associations of architects, planners and engineers in to dialogue with humanitarian and development actors. It will encourage and support changes in operational practices amongst its members. They will be involved in a range of initiatives including: aligning and improving vulnerability analysis and targeting; building the evidence base on the specifics of urban displacement and what works to meet the needs of refugees and International Development Programmes in towns and cities; surging of urban specialists (governance, planning etc) to municipalities that need it.

The way forward has to be a change in mindset, and for that change to be reflected in action in the ground. 'We are not in the field anymore' and our responses as humanitarians that are based on refugee movements in remote rural areas are not appropriate. For example if we can avoid establishing a camp in or near to an urban area, and can find dignified and locally appropriate accommodation for the displaced, shouldn't we use it?

Temporary, emergency style interventions (in shelter and provision of services) can do damage to the long-term sustainability of the economy, the urban fabric and the local society.

We have a lot to learn: we need to improve our ability with regards to supporting displaced populations dispersed across urban areas – understanding what they need, how best to communicate, finding ways to ensure they are aware of their rights and entitlements, and are safe. We are far from being about to achieve this at the moment. We don't have answers to basic questions such as: what level of support is good enough? What outcomes do we hope to achieve through this support? How much does it cost?

There are challenges, but they are also great opportunities to work differently in urban areas, and we should embrace these.

If we're going to manage this, there's a real need for humanitarian and development actors to work together. This is a general statement, but it is of particular relevance in urban areas, where not working together has serious consequences for longer-term solutions and the well-being of refugees and their hosts, and for helping urban areas absorb additional populations and maintain a stable development track.

CHALLENGES AND OPPORTUNITIES

Case Study: Italy

H.E. Mr. Inigo Lambertini, Deputy Permanent Representative of Italy to the United Nations

So far, emphasis has been placed on the impacts of migration on cities, local governments, and the associated risk of social tension. At the same time, emphasis has also been given to the role of migrants and refugees as drivers of economic growth and prosperity for host municipalities and nations. The foregoing echoes the 2030 agenda, that introduced a specific goal for cities, the Sustainable Development Goal 11, which calls for inclusive, safe, resilient, and sustainable cities.

The experience of Italy is relevant because the country is on the front lines in terms of dealing with migration flows. Each year, Italy carries on search and rescue missions that save thousands of people lost or in danger at sea—migrants in transit. But while saving lives remains the highest priority in the short-term; a long-term, comprehensive approach to mitigating crises experienced by migrants is needed. The broader approach, obviously, is to take into consideration the challenges and opportunities related to sustaining migrants and refugees. In Italy, the policy to deal with these challenges and opportunities has been characterized by close attention to the local dimension, in particular, municipalities. The diverse composition of civil society that migration triggers calls upon the local entities, including nongovernmental organizations to be adaptive, this is the Italian way.

This local dimension is important in our country because immigration in Italy is not only concentrated in larger urban contexts, as in other European countries—migrants are also settling in smaller towns or even in the countryside. Smaller population influxes facilitate integration and lower the risk of marginalization and social conflicts. Thanks to the evolution of

45

local governments and agencies, specifically with respect to agencies that facilitate welfare, health, social housing, and security, Italy has been able to develop a definitive approach and sometimes forge collaborations between sectors/municipalities on innovative policies.

Positive models of integration also include larger cities, such as Milan, whose policy welcomed over 60,000 refugees. Some small towns like the very famous island of Lampedusa or Riace, a small village located in the coastal region of Calabria, in the southern part of Italy have also played very important roles.

Riace is the best example of how challenge can be transformed into a new opportunity. In the late 90s, more and more refugees started to reach the shore of the village. The local authorities are said to have offered them job training and empty apartments, many of which had been abandoned by Riace inhabitants that had moved abroad or to Northern Italy. The influx of migrants contributed to the revitalization of the local economy and affected an increase in the local population, a critical factor in the country of Italy, which has one of the lowest birth rates in the world. For this achievement, the prestigious business magazine, Fortune, included the mayor of Riace among its top 50 world leaders. On this positive note, it is possible to consider the potential of movements of migrants and refugees as a resource for sustainable development and urbanization.

Case Study: Paterson, New Jersey, USA, and a Personal Story
Hon. Mr. Jose Torres, Mayor of Paterson, New Jersey, USA

Patterson is the third largest city in New Jersey and the county seat of Passaic County. I am the 46th mayor of Patterson, reelected for the third term in office in May of 2014. I consider myself a committed civil servant and served as mayor from 2002 until 2010 and served on city council from 1990 to 2002. I'd like to take this opportunity to share with you, a little bit about Patterson.

Alexander Hamilton founded Patterson in 1792. In the Fall of 1780, Colonel Alexander Hamilton accompanied by General Washington as his aid to camp, along with Marquise L'Enfant, and General Wayne and James McHenry, was briefly encamped along the continental army on the North side of the Passaic River between Preakness and Hawthorne. General Wayne wrote an account of the Great Falls and the fine picnic the General and his family enjoyed at the Great Falls on the Passaic River in Patterson. It is certain that Hamilton did not forget the impressive power of the 77-foot high falls, second largest in volume East of the Mississippi, for it became his chosen site for the establishment of America's first planned industrial city – Patterson - and its formation of the society of useful manufacturers, harvesting the flow of the water of the Great Falls through a system of raceways to power mills and factories of silk, locomotives, firearms, and textiles. The city became known as the Silk City as a result of the prominence of the silk industry, thus making Patterson one of the largest and most powerful cities of the Northeast.

Patterson was named after William Patterson, one of our most revered and early founders, who practiced law as an attorney for the New Jersey Supreme Court. While Governor, he supported Hamilton's charter for establishing one of the first New Jersey corporations known as the Society for Useful Manufacturers, which sought to decrease a dependence on foreign goods and help move the country from an agrarian society to an industrial society. And at its peak in the early 20th century, Patterson was the heart of the commerce and culture in Northern New Jersey. It's downtown built was one of the finest buildings of its time, especially due to the devastating great fire of 1902 in downtown Patterson. The new magnificent structure rose quickly during to the across the nation at this time and nationally prominent architects such as Charles Edwards were engaged in recreating the center city around our beautiful City Hall, which survived the fire. These edifices exemplified the financial success and wealth accumulated from 100 years of industrial growth and many of that remains today.

However the success that Patterson had is also historically placed with struggles of working class people. The city was at the center of the labor rights movement of the 19th and 20th centuries where labor unrest, focused on passing child labor laws, safety in the work place, minimum wage, and reasonable working hours. Our schools and civic and history class teaches our children that the United States is ultimately the great melting pot. Even as older generations of immigrants have moved out of Patterson, elements of the culture that they brought have remained to blend with new groups to make and enrich the city with a mixed culture of people and ideals. I'd like to think that we are not just a melting pot, but a wonderful stew – a sancocho – where every single spice is important and necessary. It is just like our diversity that makes us special and special ingredients, depending on each other in order to create the ultimately special dish that would nurture our minds and our soles. And I share this information with you, because Patterson's history has been one of open arms and open doors for many immigrants that have lived in our many neighborhoods. It is impossible therefore as a city to not welcome those seeking refuge of economic distress, that those who have been uprooted by war or are seeking religious freedom and freedom of expression.

Recently, through a house of worship the first family of Syrian refugee settled in Patterson. It is important to note that the Syrian and Arabic community have been a part of Patterson since the 19th century because besides the obvious romantic story of immigrants made good, there is also the sad undertone of being an immigrant or having to learn another language other than your own or learning to acclimate to the severity of weather or learning to trust a new government or new people. My personal story is very similar to that of many immigrants and political or economic refugees for although I am an American citizen proudly born and raised in the city of Patterson, I am also of Puerto Rican ancestry and understand the plight of many. During the time my father found difficult finding an apartment large enough to accommodate our family was compounded by overt racism of the time, where property owners would not rent apartments to spics as Puerto Ricans were called. The social service agencies of this time resolved in having my brothers and sisters separate into different foster homes. My parents would tell me that one of these foster families had tried to adopt my sisters, my twin sisters. If not for my father's courage, and the kindness of a man who offered up his apartment for my family to use, we would have never been united. This man later became our godfather.

So you see, as Mayor, I know first hand what migration and immigration means to many of us and there was no way that I could not help. As I think of identifying with H.G. Wells when he stated that we are not separate members of humanity because ultimately our true nationality is mankind. The City of Patterson has historically been a landing point for immigrant groups to the United States. Continuous waves of new immigrants have maintained Patterson's population and previous groups have moved out. Initially it was the Dutch settlers who left behind a beautiful, viral Post Office adjacent to the Passaic County Court House. The Dutch followed by the Irish, German, Jewish immigrants, followed by the Italian, Eastern European, and African-American countries. Columbia, Peru, and Dominican Republic are large numbers as well as Turkish, Arab, and Bengali families. Approximately the density is 16,823 persons per square miles. Our Board of Education Department reports that Patterson school children speak 52 different languages.

So recently, an attribute to one of our most vibrant immigrant communities, the city council just acknowledged one of our most prominent business districts as Peru Square. New Jersey's population of 1.75 million foreign-born individuals in 2016 was the 6th largest in the nation. Foreign-born account for 20.1% of the state population. Only New York and California have a higher proportion than NJ. The median income of foreign immigrants is

$26,373. In Patterson, immigrants own large shares of businesses, and newcomers help revitalize communities through small business development and general improvements to housing. Remittance far out pays foreign aid, and in 2015 a few research center reports show that they help lift people out of poverty in Latin America. Many of Patterson's immigrants are from Spanish-speaking countries and represent 54% earning. 17% of US born Latino's also maintain financial lifelines to relatives abroad.

So, in closing, it is important to know that although Patterson may not be dominated by the silk mill factory workers from before, it is enriched by the immigrant population and it was a foresight of our founding father Alexander Hamilton, himself an immigrant born out of wedlock and our country's first treasurer, that not only set Patterson on its path to greatness, but most importantly heart and humanity. We have much to be grateful for and have much faith in our future. Our crown jewel, the Great Falls, has been designated as a national park. We are positioned geographically, economically, and socially to capitalize on our many assets. They are our partners in this experience we call democracy and the City of Patterson welcomes them with open arms and open doors.

Case Study: Athens, Greece

Hon. Mr. Lefteris Papagiannakis, Vice Mayor of Athens, Greece

I know that there is a large interest in Greece and Athens. It is true, for the first time a European country is dealing with a humanitarian crisis combined with an economic and social one, but it must be remembered that in 2014, according to the UN, roughly sixty million were displaced, only one percent of them came to Europe, roughly six hundred thousand. In 2015, that figure has increased to two percent, so just over a million. It is not that big a number even if we take the number of refugees that moved to Jordan into account. I think we can bring matters into perspective.

The European Union's reaction to the recent initial influxes was to build fences and reestablish forgotten borders, generally affecting a sacrifice of human rights in order to protect its own prosperity. For me, that represents a problem. This action implies that Europe does not want to share prosperity, but rather that they prefer to keep it for themselves. And, of course, this is not the way to go for a union of over 500 million people.

We need to make brave and difficult decisions on a very large scale. We do not have to answer only to the questions of flows and management, but we need to address the root of the problem, the conflicts, which lie in the persecutions of people for their beliefs, their orientation—sexual, religious, or other—social injustice and inequality. We must also consider climate change, which seems conveniently forgotten.

The main and urgent challenge for cities is inclusion and integration for all people in society. There are choices to be made according to the possibilities – some cities will choose the housing-first approach, and some cities, the education-first approach. In Athens we have to deal with the fact that the status of Greece passed from a transit-country to a reception-country, or a destination-country. That does not change the fact that as a state, we were not prepared to face this situation. In my opinion, we also made bad political choices on the matter that cost Greece money and time.

In Athens we created accommodations during the summer of 2015 in order to house refugees who were out on the street occupying parks and public spaces and placing a lot of pressure on the municipality. We feared the state's perceived lack of action, but the mayor acknowledged that this was the minimum that Athens could do in order to safeguard the dignity of refugees and respond to our basic human obligations. We helped with approximately seven-hundred people and with the last expansion, we have reached two thousand, five hundred. In the beginning, people stayed about four or five days in Greece, transiting. And now we have people staying more than two months due to the closing of the borders in the north.

Social housing in Athens is practically nonexistent, and the same applies for Greece in general. We have two small apartment buildings to meet huge needs, which is because of our own homelessness issues. This situations becomes very difficult when compounded by refugees populations. We participate with the other partners to the UNHCR Scheme for the Relocation Beneficiaries and Asylum Seekers, offering apartments for temporary accommodation, creating twenty thousand places, along with the thirty thousand places in camps that bring us to fifty thousand accommodation places. There is no provision at the moment for social housing for refugees, an issue that we have to anticipate very quickly at a national level, but also at an international one.

We are preparing for September in order to accommodate all children in public schools, but in the long run this will not be enough. We are asked to do more with less. The cities should take it upon themselves to promote social inclusion and integration, offering the necessary and appropriate services. This action has to concern all settlements, formal and informal. The same goes for the people so we need to include undocumented people in our strategies.

In Athens we are making a big effort to prepare a strategy on integration. We participate in large networks of cities, such as Euro Cities, with which we have made a lot of efforts with respect to migration and integration. We are also trying to set up a working group on undocumented migrants with Coalition of Cities Against Racism and Discrimination, an organization that has done a lot in the area of fighting racism and discrimination along with UNICEF. Other organizations we are forging relationships with include UCLG, which helps us follow important issues, like the one we are discussing today, and Habitat3.

The mayor of Athens has launched an initiative called Solidarity Cities Networks, which promotes the role of the cities in dealing with the refugee/ migrant issue. In the years to come, over 60% of the population will be living in cities, and we need to be ready to address this new reality. Cities must be prepared to accommodate many different people, they need to be inclusive, they need to be resilient, but at the same time, they need to answer many difficult political questions and make difficult political choices. The role of cities is of global importance.

Following the EU/Turkey deal, there has been discussion about the EU making the same deal with Libya. Libya has not ratified the 1951 Convention on Refugees, and has no domestic refugee laws and procedures. It is time for the UN to take a stronger stance on this issue – protection of human rights cannot be a la carte.

Case Study: Lebanon

H.E. Dr. Nawaf Salam, Permanent Representative of Lebanon to the United Nations

As pointed out by the high-level panel on the Post-2015 development agenda: "cities are where the battle for sustainable development will be won or lost." Today the world as you know is facing the largest crisis of forced displacement since WW2. Ninety percent of refugees live in developing countries; eight aid countries host more than half of the world refugees. With one million, two hundred thousand registered city refugees, Lebanon has the highest rate of per capita refugees, two hundred thirty-two, which may explain why I'm here this afternoon. Our figures include more than four hundred thousand Palestinian refugees living in camps across the country for more than six decades.

The mass influx of refugees into Lebanon has multiplied the challenges facing my country and its urban centers, as well as its underdeveloped regions. This has overstretched originally limited resources in education, health, energy, water and sanitation infrastructures, reduced the housing capacity, increased unemployment levels, and seriously impacted economic activities and the investment climate, which has threatened their security.

Based on our national experience and the challenges we face, I am assured that the only way forward is a global shift in the approach to humanitarian assistance that expands the scope of efforts to sustain and support migrants and refugees. It is time to recognize the need to move past supplying exclusively humanitarian assistance and toward addressing the developmental needs of refugees and displaced persons, as well as host communities.

The world humanitarian summit, which convenes in Istanbul in two days, will be a major opportunity to work with all partners in this regard. Later this year, the high-level humanitarian segment of ECOSOC will continue to build on this momentum at a meeting to address large movements and migrants, which will be held in September.

The new urban agenda will no doubt be a leading inspiration to implement sustainable development goals. I look forward to hearing more input on the way forward.

Case Study: Kitchener, Canada

Hon. Mr. Berry Vrbanovic, Mayor of Kitchener, Canada

I wanted to contribute to this discussion both as a representative of United Cities and Local Governments but also the Federation of Canadian Municipalities and my own communities of the city of Kitchener and the region of Waterloo, in order to share with you some reflections on the large movements of refugees and migrants, especially in the Canadian context as it relates to our handling of the recent Syrian crisis. While my comments are focused on the recent situation and the response of Canadians, it is reflective of a pattern exhibited by

Canada for many decades: the arrival of Europeans after World
Wars I and II, as well as after the actions of the former Soviet
Union in Hungary in 1957 and the former Czechoslovakia in 1968.
In recent decades, examples include migrants, which include the
Vietnamese boat peoples, Somali refugees, those from Myanmar,
and from many other countries.

They arrived in Canada because of its inclusive and
welcoming nature, the value it places on diversity, and the
opportunities the country provided them. The conflict in the
Middle East and its human fallout has been top of mind around the
world, as you heard in the last session. It goes without saying that
the human tragedy has been tremendous and extremely
unfortunate. One fallout has been the significant amount of
refugees worldwide. We are proud to say as Canadians that
Canada's response to the Syrian refugees has been strong and
compassionate. The Canadian government committed to accepting
25,000 refugees by the end of February 2016, and in fact, as of
May, we are at about 27,000. For a country of 35 million people,
we believe this is a significant achievement in a short period of
time. The majority of these refugees have been Canadian
government-assisted refugees, however a significant amount has
been privately sponsored refugees as well. This is an important fact
because it emphasizes, in my perspective, the outlook of Canadians
on this issue. So, as much as the Canadian government's leadership
has been important in this—and quite frankly it was an issue in our
last national election last fall, and many would argue was really the
turning point that changed the results of the election—the
numbers of privately sponsored refugees, I believe, speaks about
the values that individual Canadians and local Canadian
organizations have in terms of their willingness to assist. It truly
exhibits a human and heartwarming gesture to making a difference
in the lives of their fellow people.

Of the over 27,000 Syrian refugees who have come to
Canada, approximately 11,000 of them have settled in Ontario and

over 1,200 of them in my own community, a city of over 235,000 in a region of over 550,000. At the end of April, the settlement statistics were quite significant. Almost all of them have had their government-funded health insurance fully accessible to them; over 90% of them have moved from temporary accommodations, like hotels, to stable, more permanent rental housing Canada-wide; and over 3,300 Syrian refugee children have registered for school in 27 different school boards. This speaks to the importance of integrating as well as normalizing these children so that they can do regular things like other young people their ages and really start to feel like they belong in the new country that they live in.

Accepting and settling refugees is one part of the process, although albeit very important. Another part is assessing how well refugees are settling and issues that start to emerge. This part of the process assists with better integration of refugees and really has left us with some lessons learned from our experience for future possible arrival of new Canadians. Some of the things that we observed include, with refugees getting integrated, local officials across Canada are noting particular needs with interpretation services, as well as programming. Communities are starting early to talk about discussions of Year 2 issues. Our focus with refugees is always with that initial year where they are government sponsored, but very quickly we have moved into Year 2 issues and how we can ensure that transportation and housing can be a priority going forward.

From a therapy perspective, we have seen some communities like Peterborough, as an example, that have developed some innovative programs in order to allow the newcomers to use things like art therapy to help deal with some of the things that they have been through prior to arriving in Canada. We have obviously worked in close partnership with organizations like the Canadian Red Cross, like Mennonite Central Relief, and others in terms of our handling of them. In Waterloo region, we have had many of our adult refugees integrated in terms of

programs around English competency and so on, but we find that
60% of them have 9 or fewer years of education. That in and of
itself creates some challenges, both in terms of integration,
language skill development, and ultimately their employability. We
are working to find ways to bring their skills up as quickly as
possible.

From a healthcare perspective, while we did have
healthcare needs addressed through our provincial healthcare
programs, issues such as dental care, mental health, and so on are
typically outside of the scope of that and we recognize that we need
to, particularly with this group and in the future, have more
established programs in place. There are never enough English-as-
a-second-language programs that are available, to be honest with
you.

Speaking on a local level, our community was one of 6
reception centers for resettlement of government-assisted refugees.
We quickly learned that we needed to coordinate this in a particular
fashion. In our own province, they were using an emergency
management approach to deal with this, something that typically
we would find through something the fire departments use, as an
example. While it seemed logical at the time, we found out that it
really did not work effectively and what we ended up shifting
towards was actually a community pandemic plan that we
implemented back at the time of the SARS outbreak when that
started affecting Canada. We used that plan in the various groups
around social agencies, housing agencies; the medical professions,
academia and so on, and we used those groupings in order to more
effectively deal with this issue. In fact, the model that we ended up
implementing was one that other Canadian municipalities ended up
learning from and realizing that this was an effective way for them
to deal with the refugee issue going forward. The plans that we
implemented reach out to community organizations and the
broader community to integrate their work with the government
response. The reality is for this to be effective; it cannot be

government doing this on its own. It needs to involve civil society, community organizations, and private individuals in order to assist. The number of offers of assistance that we had was unbelievable.

Going through this process, we noted that there was some frustration in the response in other areas of Canada, and so we worked with our colleagues through the Confederation of Canadian Municipalities to share best practices. In fact, we created a mayor's group of mayors across Canada, in communities that were receiving large numbers of refugees, where we could interact on a regular basis and support each other through the challenges we were dealing with. As I noted, communication was key. Social media was a big part of it, particularly in terms of bringing the community along. We developed a website: waterloowelcomesrefugees.ca. We had a twitter handle, @WRWeclomesRefugees, to go along with it, and the whole community became very engaged as part of this issue because they wanted to be part of welcoming the newcomers into our community and making a difference.

At this point, our region has settled about 1,200 refugees in total. The government has indicated that over the next couple of years, we should plan on receiving about 700 more each year, from the Syrian community in particular, for our community. I think through this experience, we have learned a variety of things and while statistics are important, really what mattered on the ground was the goodwill of the people in our community to make a difference, to be part of the solution, to welcome these new Canadians. It started certainly with our Prime Minister and our Governor General. They made this a national, nation-building effort, and I think that as other countries look at this issue, I think it is a model quite frankly that should be looked at more broadly. It is when it starts at the top and engages all these community organizations and so on that we can have the most meaningful and effective response and most importantly have the most profound impact on the lives of these individuals who have come from very troubled circumstances.

Welcoming Strategies in Legacy Cities

Mr. Nicholas Hamilton, Director of Urban Policy, The American Assembly, Columbia University

Thank you for the privilege to share some observations around the opportunities that legacy cities present to immigrants and refugees, and some of the benefits immigrants and refugees present to legacy cities. While these are complex issues, I will focus my remarks on a few success stories in cities where immigrant integration has become an important part of the new urban agenda.

I have the opportunity to work with some of the brightest minds around the nation, and around the world, working to revitalize older industrial cities--cities that have lost jobs and population as a result of shifts in the fundamental structure of the global economy and public policies.

In the US, we call these places legacy cities. These cities have not lost population because people left. Thousands of people leave big and small cities every year, and the free and regular movement of people is generally understood to be an economically beneficial process. Rather, the question is that of net migration: legacy cities are places where there have been not enough newcomers to replace those who have left. Many local governments of legacy cities see the opportunity to socially and economically integrate immigrants as a way to promote their city's vitality, in addition to attracting newcomers from within the country. At a high level, their strategy is this: a strong immigrant attraction strategy is an strong immigrant integration strategy. The social networks of individuals do much of the actual attraction.

The Case for Welcoming Strategies in Legacy Cities

Legacy cities--together with other cities and communities around the nation--are embracing an intentional "welcoming" approach: one that coordinates, institutionalizes and communicates strategies for long-term immigrant integration. Leaders and advocates in legacy cities have found a few economic, cultural and human arguments particularly helpful when establishing welcoming strategies:

Economic Arguments

The economic benefit of immigrants to legacy cities are very clear. Research by the Americas Society and the Fiscal Policy Institute have provided evidence that immigrants are essential job creators, risk takers and entrepreneurs.

- Nationally, despite comprising only 13% of population, immigrants own 28% of main street businesses; they own fully 53% of all grocery stores[1]
- Immigrants were responsible for all of the net growth in main street business nationally between 2000 and 2013[2]
- Immigrants are twice as likely to start a business than a U.S. born resident[3]
- Two examples from legacy cities:
    - Pittsburgh has a 3.4% foreign born population, while immigrants own 11% of main street businesses[4]
    - Baltimore has a 9.1% foreign born population, while immigrants own 40.4% main street businesses[5]

---

[1]http://www.as-coa.org/articles/bringing-vitality-main-street-how-immigrant-small-businesses-help-local-economies-grow
[2]http://fiscalpolicy.org/wp-content/uploads/2015/01/Bringing-Vitality-to-Main-Street1.pdf
[3]http://www.as-coa.org/articles/bringing-vitality-main-street-how-immigrant-small-businesses-help-local-economies-grow
[4]http://www.as-coa.org/articles/interactive-impact-immigrants-main-street-business-and-population-us-metro-areas
[5]http://www.as-coa.org/articles/interactive-impact-immigrants-main-street-business-and-population-us-metro-areas

These are businesses and jobs that would not exist at their scale without these new American entrepreneurs. These are businesses that provide much needed taxes and fees to legacy city governments, in addition to the goods and services they provide to the local community.

Legacy cities don't just want immigrants, they are already getting them. We all know New York City and Los Angeles are traditional gateway cities for immigrants. Indeed, a significant percentage of immigrants call them home. However, Governing Magazine found that the percentage of foreign born residents is growing at a much faster rate in many legacy cities--and other places--than it is in some of those traditional gateway cities.[6] Dayton, a mid-sized city in Ohio, has a foreign born population that jumped by 62% between 2009 and 2014.[7]

Cultural and Human Arguments

The United States, Canada and Australia are all largely nations of immigrants and their descendants. Culturally, each of these three countries were built through a long history of offering a second chance to people seeking a better life. Part of the work is about breaking down the monolithic view and inaccurate stereotypes about immigrants and refugees. It is essential to recognize that each individual is fundamentally unique, each with their own set of things they desire and can offer. To each of us it poses a personal question: are we a people who welcome newcomers like our parents, grandparents and great grandparents? Or do we close the door behind us?

---

[6]http://www.governing.com/topics/urban/gov-immigrant-friendly-cities.html#data

[7]http://www.governing.com/topics/urban/gov-immigrant-friendly-cities.html#data

Legacy Cities and Shrinking Cities in a Global Context

I will briefly mention a few points about some of the older
industrial cities outside of the US:

- Germany, which has many cities that have lost substantial
  population in the 20th and 21st centuries has a growing
  foreign born population of 11.9% and rising. Goslar and
  Leipzig have both lost substantial population. Goslar's
  Mayor Oliver Junk has been outspoken in his belief that
  immigrants should be welcomed to revitalize the city.[8]
- Australia has an uneven record. Australia is comprised of
  26.8% foreign born people[9]--that is the highest percent
  foreign born population of any nation its size (after only
  the United Arab Emirates and Saudi Arabia). While the
  world has generally seen Australia as a welcoming place,
  the last decade has seen a large shift in media and public
  tenor toward anti-immigrant sentiments. While Australia's
  older industrial cities like Newcastle have lost substantial
  population, it is only recently that the Welcoming Cities
  Australia initiative has formed and begun actively
  promoting the valuable contributions of the thousands of
  immigrants and refugees who come to Australia each year.[10]
- Australia also has a region-based fast track to permanent
  residency program that has been widely seen by analysts
  and lawmakers from both the political left and right as very
  effective.[11] Canada has a similar program.

Successful Welcoming Strategies in Legacy Cities

---

[8]http://www.theguardian.com/world/2015/aug/16/goslar-germany-we-cant-get-enough-immigrants-oliver-junk
[9]http://www.un.org/en/development/desa/population/migration/data/estimates2/estimates15.shtml
[10]https://welcomingcities.org.au/
[11]http://www.cato.org/publications/policy-analysis/state-based-visas-federalist-approach-reforming-us-immigration-policy

Legacy cities are leading the nation in making migration part of the new urban agenda. I would like to share with you a short quote by Rachel Peric, Deputy Director of Welcoming America--the leading organization in the US helping local communities be more effective at integrating immigrant communities.

> *Cities don't just become great, and then people move there –*
> *they become great because they intentionally design*
> *themselves to be places that attract and incorporate diverse*
> *people, ideas and talent, and ensure that their residents,*
> *regardless of background, can participate, thrive and belong.*[12]

While each city has taken their own approach, their actions can be categorized into three areas: public policy, collaboration with civil society, political leadership and advocacy. Each action is organized around one central theme: a strong local attraction strategy is a strong integration strategy. Social networks will do a lot of the subsequent attraction. It is worth noting this is a long term strategy, but one with short term results. It is also worth pointing out that many legacy cities share best practices in immigrant integration through the WE Global Network,[13] a collaboration of immigrant-oriented economic development initiatives from across the Midwest.

Public Policies

- Economic Development: The Migration Policy Institute estimates there are 1.6 million skilled, college educated immigrants in the US who are unemployed or underemployed. The organization Upwardly Global[14] (which has helped place 3,000 into professional careers) partners with state licensing departments to establish licensing support within specific professional fields such as

---

[12]http://www.welcomingamerica.org/news/cities-doing-more-more
[13]http://www.weglobalnetwork.org/
[14]https://www.upwardlyglobal.org/

becoming a licensed Architect, Dentist, Pharmacist, Teacher, or IT Professional.[15]

- Law Enforcement Policies: Municipal identification cards have been seen as an effective, if expensive, program in many cities. The Detroit City Council approved municipal IDs, yesterday, May 17th, 2016.[16] Many cities have also opted to enforce laws strategically. Baltimore and Philadelphia have instructed city personnel not to inquire about a person's immigration status.[17]

Collaboration with Civil Society
- Cities like Pittsburgh and Dayton have established official "offices of immigrant affairs" within the Mayor's office to coordinate public and civil society actors: including coordinating activities that celebrate diversity, promote cross-cultural interaction and combat xenophobic rhetoric.
- The national Community College Consortium for Immigrant Integration[18] offers free guides to support community colleges assist immigrants earning a workforce credential
- Universities like Rutgers University-Newark have established coalitions of universities, service providers and media through programs like their "Newest Americans" initiative which establishes new modes of storytelling around the complexities of integration.[19]
- Utica has been a national leader in refugee integration as an economic revitalization strategy. However, as a recent

---

[15]https://www.upwardlyglobal.org/skilled-immigrant-job-seekers/american-licensed-professions/michigan/michigan-professional-licensing-guides
[16]http://www.freep.com/story/news/2016/05/17/detroit-council-approves-creating-municipal-id-cards/84508736
[17]https://citiesspeak.org/2016/05/11/immigrants-and-urban-revival-in-post-industrial-america/
[18]http://www.cccie.org/
[19]http://newestamericans.com/

Next City article by urban scholar Kavitha Rajagopalan just explored, success in addressing all of the challenges presented by the variety of newcomers, has been uneven--particularly in the education realm.[20]

Political Leadership and Advocacy

- Having the city council adopt and mayor proclaim the city is a welcoming one is a big first (or second or third) step toward changing hearts and minds.
- Cities have participated with the WE Global Network and Welcoming America[21] to not only exchange best practices at the local level but also to articulate a shared vision for a national welcoming strategy.

Future Opportunities

I conclude with two interconnected points about ways that design interventions and visual media can be utilized as tools alongside existing immigrant integration tactics to both address present challenges and change established narratives.

First, there is tremendous power in design as a way to engender immigrant integration by shaping the physical world--neighborhood sidewalks, public plazas, parks--in a way that manifests the type of "welcoming" environment that many cities are working to create with the various policies and tactics I've mentioned. Consider a common urban form typology in legacy cities: a block with beautiful old houses adjacent to transportation with plenty of room for newcomers. What design options do newcomers in this context invite? In this case, design is not only about new buildings but also about utilizing older buildings that might otherwise be torn down, as in the case of the photo of this

---

[20]https://nextcity.org/features/view/refugees-us-cities-immigration-utica-new-york

[21]http://www.welcomingamerica.org/

proud new homeowner in Chadsey Condon, a very affordable neighborhood in Detroit.

Second, visual media plays a huge role in advancing immigrant integration by creating images and stories that change or disrupt dominant narratives about immigrants and refugees. Visual and creative arts are not widely practiced as an immigrant integration tool, but many smaller initiatives are beginning to use this approach. Vision Not Victim is one such project. Vision Not Victim is not a legacy city immigration integration program; it is a creative approach that supports girls and young women refugees from around the globe to articulate a vision for their own futures and provides a set of skill building programming to help them pursue that vision.[22] One product of this project is a series of photographs that capture these self-defined futures. I share one example with you today, a picture I keep on the wall of my office. It is a photograph of a young woman named Fatima who envisions being an architect to make designs that bring people joy and hopes to someday be a role model for other girls.

Architects, planners and city builders of all stripes share a core professional strength: the ability to translate ideas and dreams into focused aspirational visions that can then be built in bricks and mortar. How can designers use that practical creativity to invent new ways to change the narrative and break down the monolithic view about who immigrants and refugees are and develop new models for immigrant integration?

[22]http://www.rescue.org/vision

THE AMERICAN ASSEMBLY
COLUMBIA UNIVERSITY

LEGACY
CITIES
PARTNERSHIP

Welcoming Strategies for Legacy Cities
Large Movements of Refugees and Migrants
May 18 2016 – Nicholas Hamilton

Successful Public Policies: Professional Licensing Guides
Example: Upwardly Global and Michigan Department of Licensing and Regulatory Affairs (LARA)

IMAGE CREDIT: Upwardly Global and Michigan Department of Licensing and Regulatory Affairs (LARA)

THE AMERICAN ASSEMBLY
COLUMBIA UNIVERSITY

LEGACY
CITIES
PARTNERSHIP

Welcoming Strategies for Legacy Cities
Large Movements of Refugees and Migrants
May 18 2016 – Nicholas Hamilton

Successful Strategies: Homeownership in Detroit: Sergio
Chadsey-Condon, Detroit

IMAGE CREDIT: Beth Szurpicki, Global Detroit

LARGE MOVEMENTS OF REFUGEES AND MIGRANTS: CHALLENGES FOR SUSTAINABLE URBANIZATION

THE AMERICAN ASSEMBLY
COLUMBIA UNIVERSITY

LEGACY CITIES PARTNERSHIP

Welcoming Strategies for Legacy Cities
Large Movements of Refugees and Migrants
May 18 2016 – Nicholas Hamilton

Vision Not Victim: Fatima
AGE 16 | Future Architect | Syrian Refugee in Jordan

"It was a significant struggle for me to become an architect. For many years people told me over and over again that this is not something that a woman could achieve and they encouraged me to pursue a more "feminine" profession. But ever since I was a very little girl, I dreamt of creating buildings, making beautiful homes for families, and designs that bring people joy. Now that I have reached my vision, I hope I am a model for other young girls - showing them that you should never give up on your dream - no matter what others say."

IMAGE CREDIT: Vision not Victim, International Rescue Committee

THE AMERICAN ASSEMBLY
COLUMBIA UNIVERSITY

LEGACY CITIES PARTNERSHIP

Welcoming Strategies for Legacy Cities
Large Movements of Refugees and Migrants
May 18 2016 – Nicholas Hamilton

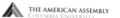

ROURCES FOR ADDITIONAL INFORMATION:

legacycities.org

legacycitydesign.org

weglobalnetwork.org

welcomingamerica.org

welcomingcities.org.au

The Refugee Issue As a Driver of Innovation in the Housing Market

Professor Floris Alkemade, Chief Government Architect, the Netherlands

The refugee crisis is causing considerable tension and unrest. The question being asked in this UN conference concerns the way in which the refugees who are admitted can integrate into our society. It is a question that those working in design and construction must also consider.

For me, an effective way to stimulate integration, is to consider the provision of reception facilities for asylum seekers in a broader context that includes other people in society who often struggle in the housing market; people such as students, first-time buyers, the elderly, and those living on their own. By looking in this way for broader social added value, we can build a more inclusive society.

I firmly believe that the targeted use of design capabilities and resources can play a key role in this regard.

As chief government architect, I am therefore mobilizing design capabilities in the Netherlands for the purpose of achieving the greater inclusion referred to. Since the total number of refugees who will have to be assisted and accommodated remains unknown, those working in design and construction are facing a unique challenge in that design work must be performed against a backdrop of uncertainty. This challenge will take a great deal of creativity to overcome.

In 2015, 1.25 million applications for asylum were submitted in the EU.[23] The Netherlands is exactly at the European average of 2.5 per 1,000 inhabitants.

There is uncertainty among people living in the immediate vicinity of planned asylum seekers' centers. They are wondering how many asylum seekers will arrive, who will be arriving, and how to handle a situation in which the actual number of arrivals far exceeds the expected number of arrivals. While discussions on the

---

[23] vluchtelingenwerk.nl.

matter are therefore never easy, at the present time in the
Netherlands, more volunteers than can be meaningfully engaged
are offering to help.

It is mainly the uncertainty about the quantity of new
asylum seekers who have been admitted which are now seeking a
home that is creating tension, because the market of affordable
homes is tight and people have often been on a waiting list for
years.

To an important extent, the refugee crisis is therefore also
a housing issue. The question in this regard is how do we add a
large number of affordable homes that can be used flexibly to the
regular housing stock for the benefit of refugees who have been
granted temporary or permanent resident status in the
Netherlands?

It is not a straightforward matter. While demand can
increase tremendously, it can also simply come to a halt.

It would therefore be logical to broaden the context and
view the issue of demand in terms of the general need for
affordable, flexible housing.

The Netherlands has a long and rich tradition in the field
of public housing. This tradition reached maturity in times of
prosperity and reconstruction; in times in which both the questions
and answers were much clearer. For the architects of today, the
complex combination of uncertain circumstances and urgent
questions is providing a wonderful and rare opportunity to
revitalize this public housing tradition. This time, however, without
a central government exercising tight control on the basis of a
welfare state ideal. Although times have changed, the social impact
of public housing has not.

As they seek to find new answers to new challenges, those
working in design and construction can embrace the influx of
refugees and the unpredictability of this influx as a driver of
innovation in this housing segment. Based on this perspective and
together with the Central Agency for the Reception of Asylum
Seekers, I set up a competition for ideas. The title was "A home
away from home." Although the competition was first and

foremost about the housing of refugees, those taking part were encouraged to think about a much broader group of people seeking homes.

We established two categories in the context of the competition: outdoor and indoor. The outdoor category concerns ideas for new, lighter forms of housing that can be temporary in nature but serve equally well as permanent accommodation because the design is such that the structure or set of structures enriches the city's urban landscape.

It is not our intention, however, to only look for solutions in terms of new buildings. The transformation of vacant buildings is also a key form of innovation. An estimated fifty million square meters are vacant in the Netherlands. Even converting only a small part of the vast amount of vacant real estate in the Netherlands into affordable, flexible homes would go a long way toward meeting the need for additional housing. My argument is therefore that the Netherlands is not full, it is empty.

The second category was therefore established to generate innovative ideas that will make it possible to use the large number of vacant office buildings, school buildings, stores, and industrial buildings, as affordable, flexible residential accommodation. Areas in our cities that are currently deteriorating because of high vacancy levels could be transformed into dynamic and attractive environments.

With respect to both categories, a limited budget is not an excuse for low quality or poor architecture. Also the proper organization of public space and the spaces that are used and shared by all population groups is of vital importance. This is also something that we must work on. Differences between population groups must be visible: interaction is required if integration is opted for.

The role and organization of the public space are of vital importance. In the context of both categories, the ways in which opportunities to integrate are promoted are therefore just as important as the innovation in a technical sense.

Almost four hundred plans were submitted, an enormous

number. In the first round, we selected six teams for both categories. With a limited budget these teams are now further developing their ideas into achievable plans. We will select six winning plans before the summer and the intention is to actually build prototypes.

The "One roof under the sun" plan, for example, combines a solar panel field with modular homes. Under this plan, one home for refugees would generate the additional energy for one single-family home in the Netherlands. The mobile "Domus Suitcase" makes it possible to create a "home" that has a kitchen, bathroom, home systems, and communication facilities within two hours. The "CLIV" project focuses on using vacant buildings for original and flexible living. This example concerns the use of vacant office space as full-fledged, permanent residential accommodation for a very affordable budget.

The underlying purpose of the competition is to encourage innovation and integration. The plans selected so far are therefore based on distinctly different approaches and have different aims. Rather than selecting a single answer, the best way to handle an uncertain context is to opt for a range of possible answers.

In conclusion, it can be said that, for the receiving community, the refugee issue is also a housing one. If we mobilize design capabilities and resources to achieve the kind of innovation in the Dutch housing market that can be applied in urban and rural contexts, we will be able to provide new and enriching solutions. The housing of refugees will then become a facet of more holistic considerations regarding the needs of a much broader group of people seeking homes. We would gain a great deal from the additional dynamics that would become possible in our cities.

Architecture has an important role to play in this crisis. The fences that close borders constitute architecture of a powerful and intimidating kind. Now, more than ever, architects must use their powers of imagination to create new possibilities and social added value.

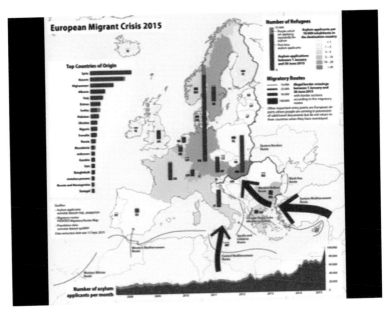

Exterior: "a roof under the sun"

DOMUSKOFFER
VAN VASTGOED NAAR FLEXGOED

PLUG & Live

Interior : "Domus Suitcase"

Interior: "Cliv"

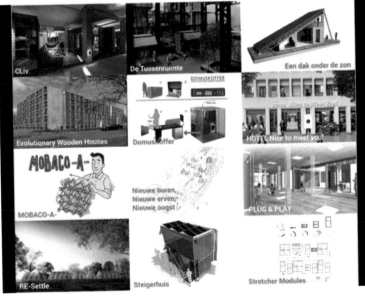

Border Greece – Macedonia, near Idomeni . march 2016

Managing Temporary and Protracted Urban Displacement as Part of Planned Urban Growth Case Study Somalia

Mr. Filiep Decorte, Deputy Director, UN-Habitat New York Office

The presentation is about the out of the box of ideas that UN-Habitat has developed over the years, focusing on managing temporarily and protected displacement as part of planned urban growth referring mostly to Somalia. Our natural counterpart for this has always been mayors and municipalities because they understand exactly what needs to be done.

A lot of professionals in UN-Habitat, including myself are architects and planners. Working in cities in conflict, we are challenged to think outside the box and, reframe the problem to come up with innovative solutions. This was the reality when I arrived in Bossaso, the North-East of Somalia in 2005.

 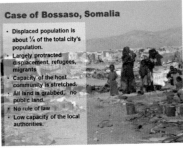

Case of Bossaso, Somalia

- Displaced population is about ¼ of the total city's population.
- Largely protracted displacement, refugees, migrants
- Capacity of the host community is stretched.
- All land is grabbed, no public land.
- No rule of law
- Low capacity of the local authorities.

Displaced represented 25% of the population. The Ambassador of Jordan was referring to 20% of people in a country, this is 25% of people in a specific city, and most of them already there for generations, while others are still arriving or passing through, people trying to migrate, or flee to Yemen and beyond. The reality of a city in conflict is one of a weak economic base, weak governance and weak capacities, with no universities, no trained planners and professionals to deal with these issues. So, we are forced to go back to the basics of what urban planning and design can offer.

Now, one of the stark realities was that 50% of these sites would burn down every year, part of them by accident, part of them on purpose, and the humanitarian system would kick in every time supplying assistance. New sticks for shelter, new buckets, new blankets.

 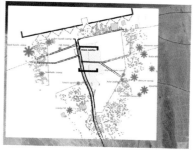

So we asked ourselves if we could deal with this differently. So as a planner we zoomed out, took the satellite image, and tried to understand, where people were? And why? We did a quick analysis, and it turned out that these people were all occupying prime lands in the fringes of the town and it was the landlords themselves that were trying to keep control of the land, and were allowing and welcoming IDP's on their site, not only to maintain their control, but also to have an income, a rental return while they were doing it.

So one of the first things we tried to do was to agree on basic regulations we can put in place. Somebody is renting in an urban area, what can he have in return? And we turned into kind of a debate at a society level in the mosques, on TV, on the radio and in the municipal council. People are renting, what are their rights? Both the host community and the IDPs were affected. It was a shared concern. Fires, lack of sanitation and related hygiene issues. So how do we address them?

We came up with simple agreements between displaced, municipality, and the landlords on what those rules were, including in terms of when the landlords want to use his land, so regulating evictions. And a simple point was also if a fire happens, we would come in very quickly with very simple re-planning, with very basic tools, just a measure tape, no plan being made almost, just a measure tape and a few drawings.

We talked about creating fire breaks, but evidently we were de-facto creating streets, and connecting those temporarily settlements with their environment, making sure the services will be able to be shared and accessible to both the host communities and the displaced. And interestingly enough, the moment we were introducing those streets we saw economical activities emerging, we saw shops being opened, we saw people becoming part of the urban fabric.

And a couple of years later some of those temporary settlements started to transform completely. Fire resistant shelters, still temporary, but at least better integrated into the environment, and no longer burning down as they were before.

There was a second big issue on the table, when we arrived. The international community, working with the government, was planning to move all IDP's, all 25%, to a site 10 kilometers out of town. A site of course with no value, but where the international community was ready to provide all the services; water, sanitation, education, health. Our answer was very simple: this will not work. We could show other places in Somalia were this had failed as people had moved back into the city, trying to remain close to their livelihood opportunities. These were people working in the port, these were people working the market, they were not going to commute, and walk 11 kilometers. They couldn't pay the transport. They were going to move back to the city to the overcrowded temporary sites which would not disappear as people keep arriving.

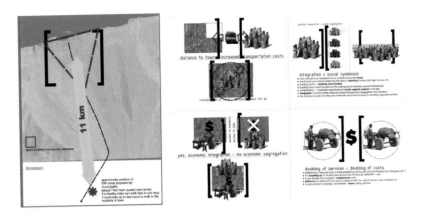

We suggested taking one step back. How do we select sites for more durable solutions for the displaced? What are the basic criteria? How can we arrive at spatial integration? We talked about affordable transport, about social integration, economic integration. We also talked about if we are going to provide those services; they have to benefit also the host community, which is equally suffering from the lack of access to water, education and health. And we turned the debate around; we shifted the discussion to talking about the city. This is one of the key messages of this presentation. We need to #ThinkUrban. If you are trying to address, specific problems affecting IDP's, refugees, and migrants, think also at the level of city. We started to talk about which direction the urban growth is going? The problems of congestion in town affecting the functioning of the port, the unsustainable linear growth along the main tarmac road. So we put forward the concept of working towards a more compact city and rethink mobility and the economic functioning of the city. So the basic concept was to re-orient the urban growth to the East, structured around a new by-pass road to the port.

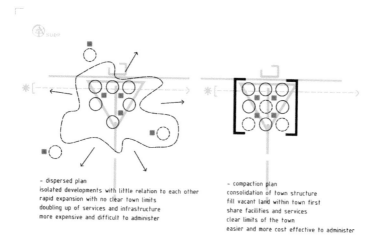

- dispersed plan
isolated developments with little relation to each other
rapid expansion with no clear town limits
doubling up of services and infrastructure
more expensive and difficult to administer

- compaction plan
consolidation of town structure
fill vacant land within town first
share facilities and services
clear limits of the town
easier and more cost effective to administer

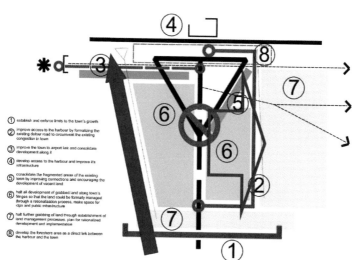

SHIFTING OF GRAVITY – the logical direction for expansion

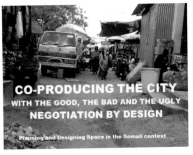 

This was not about making a plan, get it approved and implement it top down. This had to be a co-production. This is not about a planner or an architect making a drawing. It's making sure that everybody is involved in the decision making, mobilizing the investments of local people, local businesses, people that will make the difference. So negotiation by design in terms of making sure the interest of everybody and the needs of everybody were taken into account. This is not just about a building a new road, this is about making sure that we are adding city to the city, and all its components.

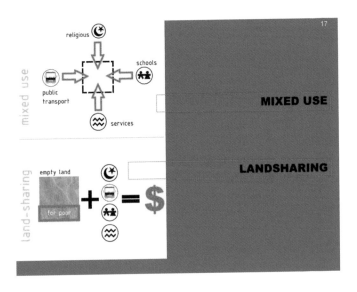

We used simple planning concepts that all could understand: mixed use, land sharing. We discussed the need to extract lands for roads and for services. The planning of the area and the introduction of trunk infrastructure and services would drastically increase the land values. In return we would extract land for roads and services and for resettlement and the integration of the displaced. A part of introducing the by-pass to the port, we tried to find solutions for other basic issues: how to redistribute the flow of goods to the port; how to re-organize the daily stream and temporary storage of life stock before being exported, how to create space for recreation and space for the youth which was as good as absent; how to deconcentrate services having multiple smaller sub-centers; ... . We talked about more efficient ways of plotting the land, which could facilitate social integration.

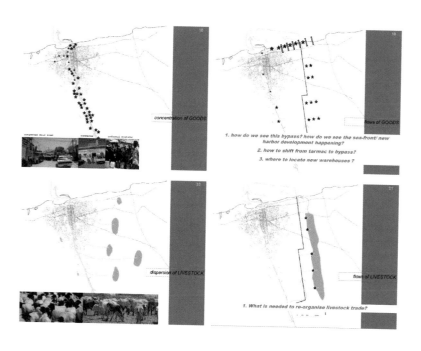

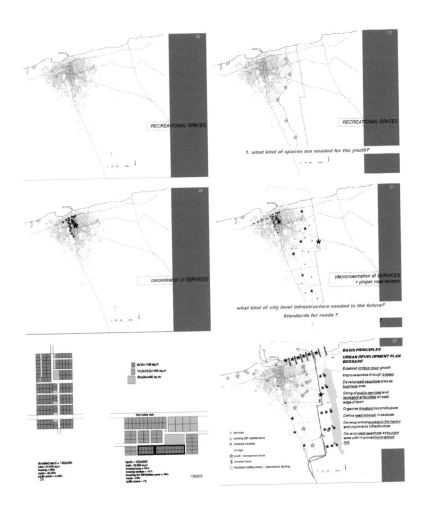

We were not talking about this in abstract, just looking at drawings. We went out, and discussed the planning ideas on the ground with council members, with engineers, with the community, trying to visualize as much as possible.

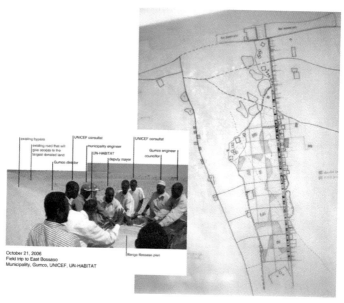

For the initial resettlements of displaced, we called for small land donations in the expansion area. Looking at small neighborhoods of 50-60 households to facilitate integration and making sure that the initial investments to connect with the road network, expand water and electricity, would help to open up the whole targeted expansion area, de-facto translating the plan on the ground. The focus was also not just on housing, but how to create and define the public space and stimulate neighborhood level economic activities.

What happened next was both fascinating and very encouraging. For the first time, displaced people started buying land, which also meant local landowners were willing to sell them, in the prime urban expansion area. Today, new warehouses are clustering around the new by-pass. This illustrated that we had created a real urban dynamic with an impact way beyond the project scope and timeline, enabling durable solutions for displaced and putting the city on a more sustainable urban growth trajectory.

This experience has contributed to UN-Habitat's big toolbox to help manage displacement as part of planned city extensions, looking at it not just as a humanitarian but also a development challenge. Similar approaches have been used in Iraq, Sudan, Afghanistan, Lebanon and elsewhere.

A final message is #ThinkUrban, use urban expertise to understand cities, what is really happening where, and why it is happening. Don't complicate things, keep it simple, come up with simple rules, simple guidance on how to plan and how to make things happen. Make sure the municipalities are involved. Even when displacement does turns out to be temporary, the foundations have been put in place for a much stronger sustainable urban trajectory. The physical assets, benefiting both host communities and displaced, are remaining. It is a way of using humanitarian interventions to leverage longer-term development.

Rethinking Refugee Communities: a Master Planning Toolkit

Mr. Don Weinreich and Ms. Eliza Montgomery, ENNEAD Lab (UNHCR-Stanford Project)

As all of us here know, refugee settlements are a response to human displacement. Displacements are nothing new; however they are occurring at a greater rate than ever before, due to conflicts, politics, economics, religious affairs and ecologic factors. Soon, climate change will exacerbate the displacement problem even further.

Too often the world views the arrival of refugees as burdensome, even threatening. But we know that amidst this tragic and terribly complicated situation of dislocation and disruption is the very real possibility for improving the lives of the refugees as well as the lives of their new neighbors. We want to turn the problem on its head and create opportunity. This is possible when humanitarian actors have the right information and the right tools, and can deploy them quickly.

In reality, informal urban settlements and camps are cities. At least the better ones are. They have in common: infrastructure, links with surrounding populations, and entrepreneurship. Their populations enjoy some degree of freedom, and movement is permitted across boundaries. What these conditions generate is opportunity, dignity and hope. But, these positive conditions are more the exception than the rule in refugee communities, particularly in isolated encampments.

We have visited refugee settlements where these conditions do exist, and they are far better than those where they do not. Design is an important factor here. Too much or too little makes a difference. When there is too little, residents will create a functional but potentially dangerous infrastructure. When there is too much the residents become disengaged. Just because a place is inhabited does not mean it is habitable. We are not alone in this thinking. The NY Times critic Michael Kimmelman has made similar observations, as have knowledgeable insiders at UNHCR, like former DHC Alex Aleinikoff and planners like Monica Noro and Werner Schellenberg.

Essential to this thesis is a redefinition of some longstanding assumptions:

1) "Refugees" are "actors" with "agency," not "burdens" waiting "idly."
2) "Hosts" are "partners" not "benefactors."

3) "Informal Settlements" and "Camps" are "cities" connected to their surroundings.
4) Humanitarian aid can be deployed to benefit both refugee settlements and partner communities.
5) Superior settlement design can be accomplished in very short time frames and at no added cost.
6) The projected lifespan of a refugee camp cannot be reliably determined and therefore the response must assume an indefinite timeframe.

As architects we are trained as "Design Thinkers" and our interest in refugee settlements comes from a long tradition of architecture helping to carry the torch of humanitarianism. We want settlement design to always strive to create opportunity for the refugee citizens. We are optimistic realists. This situation can get better. It is going to take a lot of people working together – perhaps some of you - and success will come in steps. This is why we are creating the Master Planning Toolkit – as a universal framework for all participants in the refugee response system - including refugees and hosts - to work together to create more integrated and forward looking solutions. We have all seen the results of poor planning and the failure to accept the protracted lifespan of camps. This can and must change.

When we began our work in 2012 and surveyed the existing refugee response system, we imagined that the lives of refugees and their neighbors could be better if the refugees were participants in designing their new settlements, if the refugees had the opportunity to use their own strengths and talents, if settlement plans were site- and culture-specific, if settlement designs accommodated the potential for a protracted stay, if host communities benefitted from the presence of refugees, and if the infrastructure of the settlement became a shared and permanent asset for the neighbors/hosts to make use of.

In 2013 we were invited by UNHCR to participate in the design of a new camp for Congolese refugees in Rwanda, at a site called Mugombwa. To start, we made a twelve month long. This 12-month schedule consisted of multiple design phases – site research, conceptual site zoning, and design development, as we often do as architects. We presented it to UNHCR and they said that 20,000 refugees were arriving in two months and Site work had already begun.

This moment was the birth of the Toolkit concept. We realized then that there was a burning need for fast, simple site analysis and design tools that would not only created a programmatically and environmentally functional place, but that would also identify and foster the mutual benefits and sharing of resources among refugees and partner communities while still being achievable within the constrained reality of an emergency timeframe.

This blossomed into the Master Planning Toolkit, developed with the support of UNHCR and Stanford University. It contains a system of "tools" to improve the humanitarian response and to serve as an aid to all humanitarian designers. The project grew out of an investigation and cataloguing of adaptable "good practices" and the creation of new ones where none existed. Given the brevity of this afternoon's presentation we will give you a quick overview of some of the analytical methods and the accompanying tools.

1) The first concept, which is really the backbone of all the tools is the Resource Surplus-Deficit Analyzer tool. The goal is to explicitly identifies the resources refugees can bring with them to meet the needs of host community as well as themselves. For example if an existing locale lacks schools, or wells, or medical clinics, the refugees along with accompanying humanitarian aid can provide these resources to serve both populations. This principle should drastically change the way that site selection and settlement design is executed and the tools we are developing will assist that change.

2) 2nd component is Settlement Typology Analyzer. This catalogues various settlement patterns to help planners establish appropriate strategies for settling refugees among existing communities. Note how the left hand diagram, separated settlements, is the traditional camp model. However, the toolkit emphasizes that the others, especially the urban models, are equally viable and in many cases more appropriate.
3) The Four Main Tools. Site Selection Tool. Site Analysis & Settlement Design. Measurement and Verification. The Catalogue of Good Practices.

We have witnessed the adoption of the Toolkit's principles within SSS/UNHCR in Geneva. We learned recently that SSS has created a working version of the absorption capacity analyzer tool, used to identify the effects of an incoming refugee population at their host's site, and to bridge gaps with humanitarian resources.

UNHCR's senior planners have shown a high level of interest in and support of the Toolkit, as a real-world methodology and as a means to further educate less seasoned planners.

This approach can be applied outside of the developing world, also. Our friends at The American Assembly have taken an interest in our application of the project to an existing Midwestern city with a declining population. In this instance, the refugees are located to repair gaps in the urban fabric. These cities have an abundance of underutilized infrastructure that can be used by an incoming refugee population. On the flip side, the refugees can bring a new kind of entrepreneurship to improve the city's economy. We are working on tools to define the design strategies that will foster this exchange.

That is our brief progress report on the work we've been doing for the last four years. We are very optimistic but we need your involvement to meet the promise of the project to improve the lives of refugees and their neighbors through mutually beneficial connections and sharing of resources; something that cities are especially well-positioned to do.

For the Toolkit to advance and deliver its full promise we need several things:

1) We need partners with whom to work on developing new sites and improving existing sites. These could be NGOs, the UN, or non-profit organizations.

2) We need more time in the field to define new tools and refine the ones in the Kit.

3) We need to collaborate with experts in analyzing culture, economics and public health to integrate the tools they require into the Toolkit.

We are eager to start a dialogue with anyone who sees the potential in this project; we hope to hear from you and to work on solving these problems together.

WAY FORWARD: PART I

Professor Lance Jay Brown, ACSA Distinguished Professor of Architecture, Bernard and Anne Spitzer School of Architecture, City College of New York, Consortium for Sustainable Urbanization

The thoughts, insights, and wisdom related to the extreme challenge of the current global migration and refugee crisis, the issues that have been raised and the experiences shared in this book have moved us all.

The *way forward* then, the next steps and the transfer of best practices, are all critical when considering our response to the challenges of global migration and our understanding of the opportunities as well. Of course it should also be noted and acknowledged that the host of United Nations, in New York City, on the east coast of a country is almost entirely made up of global migrants. As discussed by the Hon. Jose Torres, Mayor of Paterson, New Jersey, USA , founded in 1792 by Alexander Hamilton was started with *and remains a welcoming city of immigrants.* The United States, a country of immigrants, an experiment in immigration, could be used as a benchmark of the success possible when peoples come together for common purpose.

I want to recall and to reiterate our two key objectives of the book is to identify how large movements of refugees and migrants can be harnessed in support of sustainable urbanization, taking into account that the average displacement easily stretches over several generations; to review also innovative design and planning practices, some of which can address the critical challenges for refugees and migrants, while insuring social cohesion and equitable access to both services and housing.

I also want to further underscore and amplify that the Zero Draft of Habitat3's New Urban Agenda, the draft resolution is the call for, very specifically, a ***paradigm shift*** in our thinking, and under "Leave no one behind," states, "We recognize that international migration is a multidimensional reality of major relevance for the development of countries of origin, transit, and destination and is a phenomenon that is transforming countries, cities, and towns around the world." In this regard, paragraph 23 reiterates the need to strengthen synergies between international migration and development at all levels, I would say, much to the focus of the local level. Paragraph 24 states that "we also recognize the influx of large numbers of displaced people into towns and cities poses a variety of challenges, yet the social, economic and cultural contribution of migrants to urban life remains unrecognized, often leaving them vulnerable and excluded. And finally paragraph 41 states that "measure must be taken to counter prevailing anti-migrant sentiments such as information campaigns, capacity building, promotion of diversity, and addressing the critical role that the media plays. These strategies must be supported by well-managed migration and integration policies that promote the positive contributions of migrants." The issues of refugee and migrant societal integration and physical accommodation have been much discussed today, as has the need to counter the negative impacts of fear and xenophobia.

Let us, for a moment, acknowledge the magnitude of the challenge. At over 60 million people worldwide, displacement from conflicts is at the highest level ever recorded…...60 million!. Overall global migrants went from 148 million in 1990 to almost 230 million in 2013. And the projection for 2100 is 550 million, which would make it arguably the third largest country in the world, were it to be collected today. To quote Secretary General Ban Ki Moon's recent remarks, "We are facing the biggest refugee and displacement crisis of our time. Above all, this is not just a crisis of numbers; it is also a crisis of solidarity. When managed properly, accepting refugees is a win for everyone." Refugees are famously devoted to education and self-reliance, and as we have heard today, they bring new skills and dynamism to aging work forces.

The Consortium for Sustainable Urbanization is motivated by our concern for and commitment to improving the quality of life for all as we move deeper in to our ever-urbanizing 21st century. We "advocate for enlightened planning and design and using *a cross-sectorial approach*" and we believe in the importance of" *sustainable urbanization and resilient design* in the planning of our cities…"

The way forward is a multidimensional issue. Do we integrate peoples, do we add new communities? Is it a neighborhood, citywide, regional, or national issue? What is the way forward? It is not *the* way; it is the *many* ways, *the many different* ways that we will need to consider.

WAY FORWARD: Part II

Professor Urs Gauchat, Dean of the College of Architecture and Design, New Jersey Institute of Technology, Consortium for Sustainable Urbanization

The overriding question is: What does it take to create the political will to welcome migrants? I am not going to address the reasons for the mass migrations around the world. Nor am I going to address the moral imperatives. Instead, I will focus on what can be done in response to mass migrations. The most effective tool in our toolbox is to focus on best practices and policies that have met with success. One emphasis must be on physical planning and design and the associated services. The focus must be on solutions that will allow migrants a full life rather than mere survival. The basic premise is that forethought and careful planning could provide the best chance for societies to accommodate and integrate migrants whose lives and welfare matter.

The plight of migrants has been brought home to us in stark terms. Who can forget the picture of the drowned three-year boy old lying on the sand with waves lapping at his feet? Who can forget the never-ending river of people walking towards border crossings and who can forget the deplorable conditions in the infamous Calais Jungle in France? These images are firmly etched in our minds. These images make us feel that we have to do something and that we have to do something now.

However, when the stream of migrants ends at our own doorstep, many of these positive sentiments can change. The urge for a responsible humanitarian response can be perverted into a feeling of fear and a feeling of being threatened. This, in time, gives rise to xenophobia.

Xenophobia has become a common political response to the influx of migrants. Every time a crime is committed by a recent migrant, some politicians will extrapolate and conflate migrants and crime. This is a political phenomenon that has swept the world. Factually, migrants tend to be an economic stimulus. They are generally productive and entrepreneurial. They start more businesses than the general population on a per capita basis. I believe that the most effective way to combat a rising tide of xenophobia are successful examples, close to home, which demonstrate that migrants can have a positive influence on communities, that migrants can contribute to economic health and that migrants can be contributors.

There seems to be an ideological battle between those politicians who have an optimistic view of the influence of migrants and those politicians whose pessimistic views conflate migrant status, religion, crime and economic threat. I am reminded of a sailing analogy by William Arthur Ward:

The pessimist complains about the wind; the optimist expects it to change; the realist adjusts the sails.

Mass migrations will continue unabated for some time to come. In my opinion, the only mitigating strategy is the use of a plethora of positive examples from all continents, which demonstrate the successful integration of migrants. A positive general public opinion about migrants is a necessary precondition creating the political will to give migrants the best chance of success.

There is a difference between national policies and perceptions at the neighborhood scale. The idea that migrants have a negative impact on real estate values, create more of a demand for social services and displace the local labor force needs to be dispelled by examples, rather than rhetoric.

The design and planning community can be important participants in the transformation of public opinion. Clearly there in not one remedy that covers all misconceptions around the globe. Rather a combination of many small steps and many small examples of success are needed. There are no global solutions. In one case, the best approach might be to introduce a road with water and sanitation, whereas in another case repopulation of spare housing stock could be the answer. In yet other cases, providing a labor force for unwanted or unattractive jobs might be part of the solution. It is in this context that ingenuity; inventiveness and imagination by the planning and design community can be leveraged.

Underlying all solutions must adhere to the principals of human rights, recognition of the importance of respect and dignity and the mechanisms for integrating migrants into existing fabrics. Economic activity is the lifeblood of all populations, whether indigenous or migrant. It forms the cornerstone of community building. At the same time, new and existing communities need to be designed so that they can attract and incorporate migrant populations.

I believe that a combination of many actions - private, professional, corporate and governmental – are needed to successfully absorb migrant populations. No housing or neighborhood should be designed which stigmatizes migrants as a population within a population. Instead, the existing fabric of cities should be expanded to allow for absorption of migrant populations in a way that avoids segregation or the creation of a new underclass.

The motto for this conference might be: *Integration not Incarceration.* Migrants are people too. They expect to be treated with dignity. They expect the opportunity to work and be able to contribute as an integrated part of the community. They expect their children to be educated. They expect health care. They expect to eat, have access to potable water and working sanitary systems. In short, they expect a life that equals or exceeds the life they had before they fled.

This was not yet another conference trying to define the problem. Instead, it was a conference focused on solutions. It would be nice to think that every attendee left this conference having learnt something. Maybe there was an idea, an approach or an example, which triggered further thought and provided the motivation to do something. This conference was designed to change prevailing attitudes and to suggest that planning and forethought do indeed have an important role to play.

CONCLUSIONS

Ms. Emilia Saiz, Deputy Secretary General, UCLG

It is very important that we change mentalities on issues related to urbanization. For the cyber conversation we have been using #ThinkUrban, and there is another one that I love and want you to use: #Listen2Cities. These hash tags show that we need to involve both communities and local leaders in a different manner, and that approaches to migration crises may not be optimal or even adequate. We need to affect a change in the mentalities of people, and how people view migration. I also think we need to change the way we address pre-conflict and post-conflict situations, as well as natural disasters.

Talking about partnership is easier than actually partnering, but it is something that we will be forced to do. In that light, I want to bring to the table something that came up, perhaps with not enough emphasis—the role of associations, community associations and also local government associations. Associations are important players that can bring experiences together, cities together, and also to partner with international institutions to generate strategies to approach migration. Migration is not a bad thing. This has been said throughout the afternoon. It is a statement I will bring back home with me. I will also return home with the messages that we need to strongly advocate for mayors around the world to join the campaign against xenophobia; we need to demand strong decisions get made with respect to humanitarian issues; and we need to remember that the SDGs are calling for this type of action. SDG 11 and SDG 16 have asked local leaderships to be at the forefront of building peace and institutions to support change and accommodate migrants. These are the bases to tackle crises and migration flows, which do not necessarily need to become a crisis situations as we see happening at present.

United Cities and Local Governments, but most of all the

leaders, including local leaders, that are gathered at the United Nations in the service of governments, are called to be partners and to explore possibilities on how to learn and collaborate around this topic.

Mr. James McCullar, FAIA, VP Consortium for Sustainable Urbanization; Principal, James McCullar Architecture & Past President, AIANY Chapter

I would like to briefly summarize some of the key themes that have emerged from the conference proceedings. In spite of the alarming tragedy in the Middle East and nearly unprecedented global movement of peoples, the conference offered a new found optimism on what can be done. This was expressed in positive sound bites throughout the day, to name a few:

Think urban, think Migrant

We must leave no one behind

Integration, not incarceration

Migration can be a win-win for all

Migrants need cities, cities need migrants

Cities are at the forefront of welcoming migrants

Migrants have helped revitalize cities in decline

Migrants can sustain countries with low birth rates

The discussions integrated a range of high level perspectives with case studies or best practices from national and local levels to form a body of positive narratives. Perhaps most important, the conference focus on migration and the role of sustainable development comes at a critical juncture between major international summits that will help shape the future.

- UN Humanitarian Summit in Istanbul in May 2016

- For the first time, on September 19, the UN General Assembly will convene a summit of member states to address *The Large Movement of Refugees and Migrants*
- UN Habitat III Conference in Quito, where UN member states will adopt the New Urban Agenda to promote inclusive and stainable cities

The hope was expressed that the convergence of these summits is an opportunity to "put meat on the bones" for the earlier commitments by member states to the 2030 Agenda to bring about *more inclusive and sustainable cities*; and to bring the Habitat III and World Humanitarian communities together for a *union of urbanists and humanitarians.*

In response to the overwhelming movement of refugees and migrants to cities, the UN High Commission for Refugees (UNCHR) has shifted its policy to work closely with national and local authorities – a sure change in approach to the earlier exclusive focus on humanitarian assistance to refugee camps.

Emphasis was placed on 2030 Agenda Target 10.7 *to facilitate the orderly, safe and responsive migration at all levels.* This approach has been validated in Lebanon and Jordan, which have learned to manage large numbers of refugees relative to their populations; in Italy and Canada, where national and local policies have worked to integrate new migrants; and in Patterson, NJ, founded by Alexander Hamilton in 1792, that began and remains a welcoming city of immigrants.

Cities and local governments increasingly occupy the front line of welcoming migrants. This was demonstrated in the case study for Athens, Greece which has had to find ways to accommodate waves of new refugees through efforts at social inclusion; and by working with networks of cities to develop strategies for integration within the region.

New approaches have been pioneered by UN-Habitat to integrate displaced migrant communities in planned city extensions.

This is illustrated in the case study for Bossaso, Somalia where through careful planning with community participation, a new settlement was integrated into the existing urban context and local economy. This approach has been used in Iraq, Sudan, Afghanistan and Lebanon.

The search for jobs is a driver for immigration, with employment *a bridge between humanitarian and development responses.* This was demonstrated in Italy, where migrants have helped revitalize local industries; in U.S. Legacy Cities, where new immigrants have revitalized main street businesses; in Turkey and Jordan who have provided access to labor markets; and in Somalia where a new settlement succeeded when integrated into the local economy.

The critical role of planning and design was expressed in the challenge to seek "out of the box" solutions, which was responded to by the *"Master Planning Tool Kit"* for rethinking designs for refugee communities; a national Dutch *"Home Away from Home"* design competition for new immigrant housing; the innovative planning of Bossaso, Somalia; and a commitment from the American Institute of Architects "to step up and make a difference."

Xenophobia remains a difficult issue. It results from a fear of the unknown and poorly or unplanned migrations, which must be countered by building on positive narratives like those presented today. In Italy many migrants are settling in smaller towns or even countryside, which avoids pockets of ethic concentrations, facilitates integration, and lowers the risks of social marginalization and social conflicts. Canada has experienced similar results with the integration and social acceptance of new immigrants. These experience offer positive models of what can be achieved, but only through an integrated planning at all levels of society.

The formation of global partnerships is viewed as *a way forward* – to bring together both countries of *origin and destination, local administrations, civil society, and the private sector* to develop an understanding on how to *facilitate the orderly, safe and responsive migration at all levels.* This is a big challenge to be addressed by member states at the upcoming UN Summit on Migration and Habitat III in Quito that will adopt the New Urban Agenda. Hopefully the exchanges and emergence of positive narratives during this conference will have contributed to a better vision of what is possible.

Ms. Yamina Djacta, Director, UN-Habitat New York Office

As the Mayor of Kitchener has just said, dealing with migration challenges is a "nation building exercise". And throughout this dialogue, it was clearly demonstrated that migrants or refugees issues cannot be addressed in isolation, and that cities need to integrate and empower people of different backgrounds, including migrants and refugees, as their inclusion constitute an important element that can shape the economic, social and cultural vibrancy of cities, while also supporting respective needs of host communities and migrants.

Urbanization was viewed in the very early stages, as a challenge, as a negative, as a trend to stop and even reverse. And, now it is widely recognized that urbanization is inevitable; and that, while presenting challenges, if well planned and well managed, it offers huge opportunities; and that sustainable urbanization is a source of sustainable development. In the same way, this session has helped us look at migration from a different perspective, and develop a different narrative, a positive narrative – that, if well managed and integrated into all levels of policy making, migration provides opportunities for growth, innovation and social inclusion.

Migrants actually add value and they can really benefit the society they live in. Migrants are entrepreneurs, risk-takers and innovators, and they can reinvigorate the economy if given the opportunity - and it is about the opportunities that need to be offered. There are no easy solutions, but we also have to think out of the box; we have to come up with innovative solutions, solutions that can be tailored to the specificities of the national and local contexts in which they are applied. And this session has clearly shown that there are already such solutions around the world.

Good and enabling policies at all levels are crucial for successfully responding to the challenges and opportunities of migration At the global level, it is about solidarity among the nations; at the national level, the enabling environment, the good policies; but it is also important that, at the local level, local authorities are provided with the capacity, the resources, and the authority for successfully responding to these challenges. The relationship between migration and urban planning was also underlined.

We talked about the SDGs and the 2030 Agenda, and that is an agenda about "leaving no one behind". Migrants and refugees should not be left behind in the implementation of the sustainable development agenda for the whole of humanity. We also made the connection with the World Humanitarian Summit to be held next week, and the New Urban Agenda which will be adopted in Quito at the Habitat III conference. Also, in view of the 19th September Summit for Refugees and Migrants, we will be thinking about how to bring the rich ideas and solutions that came out of this meeting to the Summit.

UN-Habitat would like to join the Consortium for Sustainable Urbanization and all the other partners/co-organizers in thanking all the speakers, as well as the participants, for their significant contributions to this successful event, and we are looking forward to continuing this important dialogue.

ANNEX 1: SUSTAINABLE DEVELOPMENT GOALS

THE GLOBAL GOALS
For Sustainable Development

ANNEX 2 : BIOGRAPHIES

H.E. Dr. Talal Abu Ghazaleh, Chair of TAG Organization, Chair of CSU Honorary Council, and Co-Chair of Network 11

Talal Abu Ghazaleh is the chairman and founder of the Jordan-based international organization, Talal Abu-Ghazaleh Organization (TAG-Org). He has been called the godfather of Arab accounting and been credited with promoting the importance of Intellectual Property in the Arab region. Dr. Abu-Ghazaleh designed and produced TAGI TOP – a top of the line laptop with the portability of a netbook. His Knowledge Society is one of the foremost initiatives by HE Senator Talal Abu-Ghazaleh that empowers young Arabs under the TAG-Org's corporate responsibility. He has published multiple dictionaries: Dr. Abu-Ghazaleh has received many honors, including: Social responsibility awards launched by CSR Regional Network for his work in social initiatives (Kingdom of Bahrain, 2014), Man of the Year Award from Palestine International Institute (Amman, 2012), Honorary Award from the Arab Federation for the Protection of Intellectual Property Rights (Jordan, 2009), The International Lifetime Achievement Award (Dubai, 2008), IP Hall of Fame Inductee in the IP Hall of Fame Academy (Chicago, USA, 2007), Honorary Doctor of humane Letters (Canisius College, New York, 1988), Decoration of the Republic of Tunisia (1985), Chevalier de la Legion d'honneur (France, 1985), etc. Besides being the chair of the Honorary Council of the Consortium for Sustainable Urbanization, Dr. Abu-Ghazaleh has been chair of Global Alliance for ICT and Development (2009-2010), and many others.

Professor Floris Alkemade, Chief Government Architect, the Netherlands

Floris Alkemade is Chief Government Architect (Rijksbouwmeester) as of 1 September 2015. The Chief Government Architect protects the architectural quality of the Dutch state property and their incorporation into the urban area as a whole. He is a Dutch architect, urban designer and former partner of Office for Metropolitan Architecture (OMA). He gives lectures and seminars at universities in the Netherlands, Belgium and France. In August 2006, he opened his own office and is currently director of FAA and FAA/XDGA. He works on complex projects both within the Netherlands and abroad. He stands out due to his attention for infrastructure and logistics, as shown by the area development and incorporation of the TGV station in the center of the French city of Lille, as well as studies for the A12 and other Dutch motorways. Themes such as rezoning and urban development are also an important part of his work.

Professor Lance Jay Brown, ACSA Distinguished Professor of Architecture, Bernard and Anne Spitzer School of Architecture, City College of New York; Consortium for Sustainable Urbanization

Lance Jay Brown, FAIA, DPACSA, is an architect, urban designer, educator, and author. He is an ACSA Distinguished Professor in the Bernard and Anne Spitzer School of Architecture, City College of New York, CUNY, served as assistant director of the Design Arts Program at the NEA and as advisor to the World Trade Center Site 9/11 International Memorial Design Competition and Boston's Logan International Airport 9/11 memorial Competition. His numerous awards include: AIA New York State President's Award for Excellence in Non-traditional Architecture and the prestigious AIA/ACSA Topaz Medallion for Excellence in Architectural Education. He served on the board of the AIANY Chapter, is founding Co-Chair of the AIA Design for Risk and

Reconstruction Committee, and founding Board member of the Consortium for Sustainable Urbanization.

Ms. Emilia Sáiz Carrancedo, Deputy Secretary General, UCLG

Emilia Saiz is Deputy Secretary General of United Cities and Local Governments based in Barcelona, Spain. In 2004 she moved to Barcelona contributing to the set up of United Cities and Local Governments where she has fulfilled several posts, Director of Statutory Affairs, Director of Statutory Issues and Institutional Relations and Chief of Staff before coming Deputy Secretary General. She joint the international municipal movement in 1997 at the International Union of Local Authorities, one founding organization of UCLG, based in The Hague, where she worked in projects dedicated to institutional capacity building of local governments associations and the promotion of gender equality in local governments, as Director of Programmes. She has a Master of Arts in European Studies with specialization in International and Dutch Law.

Dr. Aliye Pekin Çelik, President, Consortium for Sustainable Urbanization

Aliye Pekin Çelik, is the President and founding member of the Consortium for Sustainable Urbanization. She was instrumental in establishing innovative participatory mechanisms to build alliances as the Chief of Economic and Social and Inter-organizational Cooperation Branch, UNDESA.. As the Head of New York office and in her career at UNHABITAT, she focused on sustainable urbanization, energy, housing and gender issues. Previously she was a principal researcher in the Building Research Institute in Turkey. She has bachelor and master degrees in architecture from Middle East Technical University, M.F.A. in Architecture from Princeton University, and a PhD from Istanbul Technical University. Çelik was a Fulbright Scholar and received numerous awards from OECD, Princeton University, American

Institute of Architects and Soroptimist International NYC, where she served as President. She is the representative of the United Cities and Local Governments to the United Nations.

Dr. Joan Clos, Under-Secretary-General and Executive Director, United Nations Human Settlements Programme (UN-Habitat) and Secretary-General of the Habitat III Conference

Joan Clos is the Executive Director and Under Secretary General of the United Nations Human Settlements Program (UN-Habitat) since October 2010. He was twice elected Mayor of Barcelona, serving two terms from 1997 until 2006. He was Minister of Industry, Tourism, and Trade of Spain between 2006 and 2008. Prior to joining the United Nations, he served as the Spanish Ambassador to Turkey and Azerbaijan. At the international level, in 1998 he was elected President of Metropolis, the international network of cities. Two years later, he was elected President of the World Association of Cities and Local Authorities (WACLAC). Between 2000 and 2007, he served as the Chairman of the United Nations Advisory Committee of Local Authorities (UNACLA). And between 1997 and 2003, he was member of the Council of European Municipalities and Regions (CEMR). Dr. Clos received a number of awards, including a gold medal from the Royal Institute of British Architects in 1999 for transforming Barcelona. In 2002, he won the UN-Habitat Scroll of Honor Award for encouraging global cooperation between local authorities and the United Nations. He is a medical doctor with a distinguished career in public service and diplomacy.

Mr. Filiep Decorte, Deputy Director, UN-Habitat New York Office

Filiep Decorte is currently the Deputy Director of UN-Habitat's New York Liaison Office. Previously, he was the chief technical advisor and the focal point for UN-Habitat's crisis-related work in New York. He played a key role in developing an urban track towards the

World Humanitarian Summit and the emerging Global Alliance for Urban Crises. During his career, he has predominantly focused on urban initiatives in conflict- and crisis-affected countries, specializing in urban planning, land, and housing issues. He has worked for UN-Habitat for more than fifteen years in different capacities, including long-term assignments in Haiti, the occupied Palestinian territory, Somalia, and Morocco. He also acted as coordinator for UN-Habitat's Global Disaster Management Program. He was trained as a civil engineer, architect, and urban and regional planner with advanced master's degrees from the Universities of Ghent and Leuven in Belgium.

Ms.Yamina Djacta, Director, UN-Habitat New York Office

Yamina Djacta, Director, UN-Habitat New York Office. She has been working in the areas of policy analysis, planning, programme development, management, capacity development, as well as monitoring and evaluation for over 30 years at the national and international level. Her career with the United Nations began at the United Nations Development Programme (UNDP) in the area of public administration modernization and capacity development, with a focus on francophone Africa. She then joined UN-Habitat, serving in various positions working on urban issues within UN-Habitat, in Nairobi as well as in New York. Ms. Yamina Djacta holds a "Licence en sciences économiques" and a Master of Business Administration (MBA), with a major on International Management. She also undertook post-graduate studies in Corporate Finance.

Dr. Lucy Earle, Urban Advisor, International Rescue Committee

Lucy Earle is an urban adviser for the International Rescue Committee's Urban Crises Learning and Advocacy Project and a co-lead of the Urban Expert Group for the World Humanitarian Summit. She is seconded from the Department for International Development (DFID) - UK to IRC as part of the Urban Crises Learning and

112

Advocacy Partnership. After completing an MA in Social Development at the Institute of Latin American Studies, University of London, Lucy moved to Rio de Janeiro, where she worked in the projects department of ActionAid Brasil. She left the *cidade maravilhosa* in March 2002 to join UNRISD as a research assistant on the Civil Society and Social Movements Programme. She has conducted field research in Cuba for her MA thesis on the housing crisis in Havana and has worked and studied in Mexico and Chile.

H.E. Mr. Jan Eliasson, Deputy-Secretary-General of the United Nations

Jan Eliasson was appointed Deputy-Secretary-General of the United Nations by Secretary-General Ban Ki-moon (On 2 March 2012). He took office as Deputy Secretary-General on 1 July 2012. He was from 2007-2008 the Special Envoy of the UN Secretary-General for Darfur. Prior to this, he served as President of the 60th session of the UN General Assembly. He was Sweden's Ambassador to the US from September 2000 until July 2005. In March 2006, Mr. Eliasson was appointed Foreign Minister of Sweden and served in this capacity until the elections in the fall of 2006. From 1980 to 2000, he served many key positions, and was the first UN Under-Secretary-General for Humanitarian Affairs.

Professor Urs Gauchat, Dean of the College of Architecture and Design, New Jersey Institute of Technology (NJIT); Consortium for Sustainable Urbanization

Urs Gauchat is the Dean of the College of Architecture and Design and Professor of Architecture, New Jersey Institute of Technology. Professor Gauchat transformed the School into an internationally recognized leader in the area of CAD (Computer Aided Design) and community development. He is particularly interested in creating a bridge between the considerable resources of universities and the needs of communities. As a professional and academic he has a long-standing interest and expertise in the field of housing and community building worldwide. From 1978-1998, Professor Gauchat was the President of Gauchat Architects, Inc. He also served as a consultant to governmental and nongovernmental agencies. Professor Gauchat holds a Master in Architecture from the Harvard Graduate school of Design.

Mr.Nicholas Hamilton, Director of Urban Policy, The American Assembly

Nicholas Hamilton, Director of Urban Policy of The American Assembly where he leads the Legacy Cities Partnership, a national coalition of practitioners, researchers and leaders working to revitalize America's legacy cities. His work focuses on economic development, urban governance, and civic engagement. Prior to joining The Assembly, he worked at the Earth Institute Center for Sustainable Urban Development at Columbia University. His architectural and urban design work for the firm Davis Brody Bond included the master planning and architectural design of US diplomatic facilities abroad to the design and construction management of research laboratories at Columbia University. Mr. Hamilton holds a Masters of International Affairs from Columbia University's School of International and Public Affairs and BA in Architecture from the University of California at Berkeley.

Mr. Fabrizio Hochschild, Deputy to the SG's Special Advisor for the Summit on Addressing Large Movements of Refugees and Migrants

Fabrizio Hochschild is Deputy to the SG's Special Advisor for the Summit on Addressing Large Movements of Refugees and Migrants. He was UN Resident and Humanitarian Coordinator in Colombia. Previously, he was Director of Human Resources Department of Support FALD UN (2010-2013); Chief of the Division of Field Operations and Technical Cooperation of the United Nations High Commissioner for Human Rights Human in Geneva (2005-2009). He held several positions with the United

Nations High Commissioner for Refugees (UNHCR) in Tanzania, Belgrade, and Bosnia-Herzegovina and Croatia. He worked also for United Nations Refugees Works Agency (UNRWA) in the West Bank (1990-1991). Between 1997 and 2000 he was special assistant to the Assistant Secretary-General UN, Sergio Vieira de Mello, in Geneva UNHCR, OCHA New York and peacekeeping missions in Kosovo (UNMIK) and East Timor (UNTAET). He has an MA in literature and languages (Spanish and German) at Magdalen College, Oxford and MSc in forestry and Land Management St. Antony's College, also in Oxford.

H.E. Mr. Sven Jurgenson, Vice-President of ECOSOC and Permanent Representative of Estonia to the United Nations

Sven Jürgenson, is the new Permanent Representative of Estonia to the United Nations. Prior to his appointment, he was his country's ambassador to France and Monaco, from 2010, during which time he also served as Permanent Representative to the Organization for Economic Cooperation and Development. He served as Foreign Policy Adviser to the President from 2006 to 2010, and from 2003 to 2006, as Under-Secretary for Political Affairs at the Ministry of Foreign Affairs. Mr. Jürgenson holds a master's degree from Tallinn Polytechnic Institute in data processing and pursued further studies in that field at Ingenieurhochschule Dresden, in Germany.

H.E. Ms. Dina Kawar, Representative Jordan to the United Nations and co-facilitator for the UN General Assembly High-Level Meeting on addressing large movements of refugees and migrants

Dina Kawar is the new Permanent Representative of Jordan. Prior to her appointment, she was Ambassador of Jordan to France from 2001 to 2013, with concurrent accreditation to the United Nations Educational, Scientific and Cultural Organization (UNESCO) and to the Holy See, since 2002. From 2005 to 2013, she also served as Ambassador to Portugal. From 2000 to 2001, Ms. Kawar was Director of Bureau Privé de Sa Majesté le Roi Abdullah II in Paris, France, having previously headed the Paris office of the Bureau de S.A.R Prince El Hassan from 1991 to 2000. From 1985 to 1990 she served in the Bureau's Amman office. She holds a master's degree in international affairs from Columbia University and a bachelor's degree in international relations from Mills College, both in the United States.

Ms. Ninette Kelley, Director, NY Office, UNHCR

Ninette Kelley is the Director of UNHCR's Liaison Office in New York since August 1st 2015. She joined UNHCR in 2002 and has served in several senior management positions both at Headquarters and in the field. Prior to her assignment in New York, Kelley served five years as UNHCR's Representative in Lebanon, leading one of UNHCR's most complex refugee operations. Before joining UNHCR, Kelley served for 8 years with the Immigration and Refugee Board (IRB) of Canada as a member of the Convention Refugee Determination Division (CRDD) and of the Immigration Appeal Division from June 1994 to June 2002. Previously she held various policy and consultative roles with international humanitarian agencies focusing on development and refugee issues. She is the author of *The Making of the Mosaic: The History of Canadian Immigration Policy*, University of Toronto Press, 2nd edition, October 2010 (with Michael Trebilcock) and has published in the areas of human rights law, citizenship, refugee protection, gender related persecution and the Canadian Charter of Rights and Freedom. She is a lawyer by training.

Ms. Michele Klein-Solomon, Director of the Secretariat of Migrants in Countries in Crisis International Organization for Migration

Michele Klein Solomon is Director of the Migration Policy and Research Department at the International Organization for Migration (IOM), where she has been instrumental in building the Organization's migration policy expertise and profile, including by helping to create and leading the IOM International Dialogue on Migration, and serving as a key member of the secretariat to and producing the Berne Initiative's International Agenda on Migration Management. Ms. Klein Solomon received her Juris Doctor and Masters of Science in Foreign Service (MSFS) degrees, cum laude, from the Georgetown University Law Center and Georgetown University School of Foreign Service, in 1988, with honors including the Landegger Honors Certificate in International Business Diplomacy. She served as the topics editor for the journal Law and Policy in International Business. Prior to joining IOM in 2000, Ms. Klein Solomon served as an Attorney Adviser with the U.S. Department of State, Office of the Legal Adviser, from 1989 - 2000. She served in a number of offices (UN Affairs, Law Enforcement and Intelligence, Human Rights and Refugees, and Management) during her tenure with the State Department. Of particular relevance to her current position, Ms. Klein Solomon served as the Department's principal refugee and migration lawyer from 1991 - 1996.

H.E. Mr. Inigo Lambertini, Deputy Permanent Representative of Italy to the United Nations

Inigo Lambertini was appointed Deputy Permanent Representative of Italy to the United Nations in January 2014. From 2010, Ambassador Lambertini served four years as Principal Director for Country Promotion at the Italian Foreign Ministry in Rome. Before that he was appointed Advisor to the Secretary-General of the Foreign Ministry for Economic Diplomacy (2009-10). Between 2005 and 2009 he served as Deputy Permanent Representative of Italy to the OECD in Paris. He served as Counselor on Domestic Policy at the Embassy of Italy in Washington and subsequently First Counselor (2001-05). In the previous decade, he served in various offices, such as Counselor of the permanent mission, Head of the Commercial Office at the Embassy of Italy, and many others. He obtained a degree in Law cum laude from Universita' Federico II in Naples (1983).

Ms. Carol Loewenson, President of AIA NY Chapter, Partner, Mitchell, Giurgola Architects

Carol Loewenson, FAIA is a partner at Mitchell/Giurgola Architects and is the current President of AIA New York. She has served as a Board member of the Center for Arts Education, the Center for Architecture Foundation and New Yorkers for Parks. In addition, she has served on numerous local and national professional panels and juries. She earned a Bachelor of Arts degree from Barnard College and a Master of Architecture degree from Columbia University. She was elected to the College of Fellows of the American Institute of Architects in 2013.

Eliza Montgomery, ENNEAD Lab

Eliza Montgomery was part of the design team that collaborated to produce a toolkit to help authorities site and design refugee settlements in a way that improves quality of life and creates beneficial connections with host communities. Additionally, she presented with Don Weinreich, *Rethinking Refugee Communities* as part of an evening's look at the refugee crisis sponsored by Arcam (The Amsterdam Centre for Architecture) and the Academy of Architecture in Amsterdam along with Hans van der Made, an Amsterdam-based architect involved with the Jordanian Al Zaatari camp. She attained a Master in Architecture, from Columbia University.

H.E. Mr. Michel Tommo Monthe, Acting President, United Nations General Assembly; Representative of Cameroun to the United Nations

Michel Tommo Monthe of Cameroon was elected Chair of the Third Committee (Social, Humanitarian and Cultural) on 27 August 2010. He was named his country's Permanent Representative to the United Nations on 8 September 2008. Prior to that appointment, he served as Vice-Chairman of the Advisory Committee on Administrative and Budgetary Questions (ACABQ) from 2006. Before that, he was Special Adviser to the President of the fifty-ninth session of the General Assembly from 2004 to 2005. From 1996 until 2004, he was Inspector General in Cameroon's Ministry of External Relations, responsible for inspections of central services, diplomatic missions and consulates abroad, as well as coordinator of all files relating to multilateral cooperation, particularly those relating to the United Nations. He holds Bachelor of Arts and Master of Arts degrees from the University of Yaoundé, Cameroon, as well as a doctorate in international relations from the International Relations Institute of Cameroon, University of Yaoundé II.

Mr.James McCullar, FAIA, VP Consortium for Sustainable Urbanization, Past President, AIANY Chapter

James McCullar, FAIA, is Vice-President of the Consortium for Sustainable Urbanization and principal of James McCullar Architecture in New York City. His work in community design and affordable housing has been recognized through numerous awards, including a national AIA Honor Award in urban design for the Jamaica Market and election to the AIA College of Fellows. In 2008 he served as President of AIA New York, where he led the chapter's response to Mayor Bloomberg's initiatives for PlaNYC, which included collaborations for the UN Forum on Sustainable Urbanization in the Information Age and the Greening the Iron Ribbon Conference on the Northeast Megaregion. From 2003 to 2006 in response to the Mayor's housing initiatives, he led a forum that showcased housing design at the Center for Architecture in New York. As a founding member of the Consortium for Sustainable Urbanization, he has been engaged in developing collaborations for programs with UN Habitat on emerging issues. He has taught at Kansas State University and the New Jersey School Institute of Technology. He received a BA and BArch from Rice University, a Fulbright for urban design in Paris, France, and a Masters in Architecture from Columbia University where his thesis was on New York region.

Hon. Lefteris Papagiannakis, Vice Mayor of Athens, Greece

Lefteris Papagiannakis, Vice Mayor of Athens. He was born in France in 1971. Studied law in the university of Lille II and worked in the European Parliament. He is a member of the Athens municipal council and president of the Immigrant Integration Council.

Mr. Vinícius Carvalho Pinheiro, Special Representative to the UN and Director ILO Office for the United Nations

Vinícius Carvalho Pinheiro, is the Deputy Director of the ILO Office for the United Nations (New York) and Executive Secretary of the Social Protection Interagency Coordination Board since October 2012. Before moving to New York, he served as senior social protection adviser to the ILO Director General in Geneva. He also acted as ILO Sherpa to the G20 Development Working Group and served as Executive Secretary of the Social Protection Floor Advisory Group. Prior to joining the ILO, he was the National Secretary for Social Security of Brazil (1999 -2002) responsible for designing and implementing the Brazilian Pension reform. In 2001, he was elected Vice-President of the Inter-American Social Security Conference. Between 2002 and 2005 he worked in the Organization for Economic Cooperation and Development (OECD), in Paris and also provided consultancy services for the Inter-American Development Bank (IDB) and to the World Bank in projects in Africa and Latin America.

Ms. Lakshmi Puri, Assistant Secretary-General, UN Women, Global Migration Group Chair 2016

Lakshmi Puri is Assistant Secretary-General of the United Nations and Deputy Executive Director of UN Women. She is directly responsible for the leadership and management of the Bureau for Intergovernmental Support, UN System Coordination, and Strategic Partnerships. Ms. Puri

joined UN Women in March 2011 and was the interim head of UN
Women from March to August 2013. Prior to joining UN Women,
she was Director of the UN Office of the High Representative for
the Least Developed Countries, Landlocked Developing Countries
and Small Island Developing States. She joined the United Nations
in 2002 as Director of the largest division at the United Nations
Conference on Trade and Development (UNCTAD), the Division
of International Trade in Goods, Services and Commodities. From
2007 to 2009, she served as UNCTAD's Acting Deputy Secretary-
General. She has a Bachelor of Arts (honors) from Delhi
University and a postgraduate degree from Punjab University, as
well as professional diplomas.

Mr.James Roig, Secretary-General, United Cities and Local Governments

Josep Roig has held the post of Secretary General
of United Cities and Local Governments since
September 2011. He was a founding member of
Metropolis, the metropolitan section of UCLG,
in 1985, becoming Secretary General of the
organization in 1999. Previously, he had worked
in the Barcelona Metropolitan Corporation (1983-
1990, 1996-2000, 2009-2011), in different positions on economic
promotion, asset management, finances and planning, first as
Coordinator of Technological and Industrial Parks, then as Deputy
Director and, finally, as Financial Director and Deputy Director
General. Josep Roig has held the posts of lecturer in Urban and
Regional Planning at the Department of Economics of the
University of Barcelona (1977-1985) and Director General of the
University of Barcelona (1990-1994). Graduated in economics by
the University of Barcelona (1967-1972) and Fulbright Scholarship
at the University of Southern California (1974-1977).

H.E. Dr. Nawaf Salam, Permanent Representative of Lebanon to the United Nations

Nawaf A. Salam, the new Permanent Representative of Lebanon to the United Nations (July 2007). Prior to his appointment, Mr. Salam served as Chair of the Political Studies and Public Administration Department at the American University of Beirut, taking leave as of February 2007. A Visiting Associate Professor of Political Science from 2003 to 2005, he also worked as a part-time lecturer at the institution while busy with his private law practice between 1992 and 2003. From 1989 to 1992, Mr. Salam was a foreign legal consultant at the law firm of Edwards & Angell in Boston, Massachusetts. He has been an associate researcher at the Centre d'histoire de l'Islam contemporain at the Sorbonne University in Paris and holds degrees from the Institut d'Etudes Politiques in Paris, Harvard Law School, and Beirut's Lebanese University and the Sorbonne University in Paris. Proficient in Arabic, English and French, Mr. Salam co-authored the draft law submitted by the Special Electoral Law Commission to the Government of Lebanon in June 2006, in addition to drafting and editing a related report of the Commission.

Ms. Ashley Simone, Fellow, Consortium for Sustainable Urbanization

Ashley Simone is a New York City based photographer, designer, editor and educator. She received an M.Arch from the Graduate School of Architecture, Planning and Preservation, Columbia University and teaches in the School of Architecture at Pratt Institute. She is a member of the GSAPP/NEW INC. Incubator at the New Museum. Her recent editorial work includes the books A Genealogy of Modern Architecture: Comparative Critical Analysis of Built Form by Kenneth Frampton (2015), Absurd Thinking between Art and Design by Allan Wexler (2016), and Two Journeys by Michael Webb.

Hon. Jose Torres, Mayor of Patterson, New Jersey, USA

Jose 'Joey' Torres is the 46th Mayor of the City of Paterson, re-elected for a third term in office in May 2014. His term has been highlighted by economic growth initiatives, improving constituent services and his administration's "Investment in Human Capital" program, culminating in the "Safe City Initiative," a partnership with John Jay College of Criminal justice. A committed civil servant, he was elected Mayor of the City of Paterson in 2002 and 2006 and served in the City Council since 1990. During his first two terms as Mayor he established hundreds of affordable housing units for working families, and established twenty-one (21) after-school centers. Along with Governor James E. McGreevey, he announced the designation of the Paterson Great Falls as a State Park later being intrinsically involved in its designation as the Paterson Great Falls National Historical Park. He has also participated in the Mayor's Institute on City Design in South Carolina and served as a panelist in the International Association of Chiefs of Police (ICAP). Mayor Torres is a recipient of the New Jersey Planning Association's Award for Smart Growth/City of Paterson's Master Plan and serves on the Board of Directors of Preservation New Jersey.

Mr. Frederic Vallier, Secretary General of the Council of European Municipalities and Regions

Frédéric Vallier is Secretary General of the Council of European Municipalities and Regions (CEMR) since 1 February 2010. He has over twenty years of experience working with local and regional authorities, including within the city and Metropolitan Authority of Nantes (France) where, from 2004 to 2010, he held the position of Deputy-head of the Mayor's office, advisor for international and European affairs, and Head of the European Service. From 2003 to 2008, he was successively in charge of cross-border cooperation in a Department of Lorraine, Adviser in the field of "development and international relations", after which he was appointed Deputy-head of the cabinet of the mayor of Nantes,

Jean-Marc Ayrault. In 1995, he was elected Deputy-Mayor of Fresnes, a municipality in the south of Paris. He holds an Executive Master's Degree in public management from Science Po Paris. In 2012, he was elected member of the board of the European Movement International.

Hon. Mr. Berry Vrbanovic, Mayor of Kitchener, Canada

Berry Vrbanovic was elected as Mayor of the City of Kitchener in 2014, after serving as a City Councillor from 1994-2014. During his time as a councillor, Berry's commitment to his constituents resulted in the fire station at Ottawa Street and River Road, the Grand River-Stanley Park branch of the Kitchener Public Library and the Stanley Park Community Centre. In addition to serving on all regular standing committees of Kitchener city council and Region of Waterloo council, Berry is also an appointee and active participant on many boards and committees. He is also Treasurer of United Cities & Local Governments and is President Emeritus (2011-12) of the Federation of Canadian Municipalities. In 2014, Berry ran for the elected office of mayor and with an outpouring of community support was successful. He is committed to improving the quality of life for residents in Kitchener and throughout the Region of Waterloo.

Mr. Don Weinreich, ENNEAD Lab (UNHCR-Stanford Project)

Don Weinreich is a partner at Ennead Architects, where his work on award-winning projects spans over 25 years. In addition to his project-related responsibilities, his efforts are directed toward promoting an integrated practice of design excellence supported by technical innovation and a collaborative team-based project management culture. In collaboration with the United Nations High Commissioner for Refugees (U.N.H.C.R.) and Stanford University, Mr. Weinreich is currently leading the Ennead Lab research project Toward a Unified approach, developing a new methodology for the planning and design of refugee settlements.

He graduated from Columbia College and earned his Master of
Architecture from Columbia University's Graduate School of
Architecture, Planning and Preservation. He is a LEED Accredited
Professional and a member of the American Institute of Architects.

Dr. H. Öner Yurtseven, Consortium for Sustainable Urbanization

H. Öner Yurtseven is Professor Emeritus of
Electrical and Computer Engineering and Dean
Emeritus of the School of Engineering and
Technology, IUPUI. He has extensive
experience in teaching, research, and academic
administrative work. His specialty areas are
robotics, signal processing, international
engineering and technology education, and engineering and
technology accreditation. His current interests are photovoltaic
energy, electric transportation systems, and carbon credit markets.
He is a board member of CSU, EarthSolar Technologies, and
Electricore. He has BSEE degree from the Middle East Technical
University, Turkey and PhD degree from the Johns Hopkins
University, USA.

ANNEX 3: 18 MAY 2016 MEETING AGENDA

Permanent Mission of Italy to the United Nations, UN-Habitat, UNHCR, IOM, ILO, UCLG, UN-Women / Global Migration Group Chair 2016, Consortium for Sustainable Urbanization (CSU), American Institute of Architects -NY Chapter, Network 11

Large Movements of Refugees and Migrants: Critical Challenges for Sustainable Urbanization

Agenda 18 May 2016

ECOSOC Chamber New York, NY 2.00pm-6.00pm

1.00 pm   Registration

2.00 pm   **Opening statements**

H.E. Mr. Jan Eliasson, Deputy-Secretary-General of the United Nations

H.E Mr. Michel Tommo Monthe Acting President, United Nations General Assembly; Representative of Cameroun to the United Nations

H.E. Mr. Sven Jurgenson, Vice-President of ECOSOC and Permanent Representative of Estonia to the United Nations

H.E. Ms. Dina Kawar, Representative Jordan to the United Nations and co-facilitator for the UN General Assembly High-Level Meeting on addressing large movements of refugees and migrants

Mr. Josep Roig, Secretary-General, United Cities and Local Governments

Ms. Lakshmi Puri, Assistant Secretary-General, UN Women, Global Migration Group Chair 2016

2.30 pm   **Keynote for the High Level Summit on Migrants
and Refugees 19 September 2016**

Dr. Joan Clos, Under-Secretary-General and Executive
Director, United Nations Human Settlements
Programme (UN-Habitat) and Secretary-General of the
Habitat III Conference

2.45 pm   **Dialogue Session I: Challenges and opportunities**

Chair: **H.E. Inigo Lambertini**, Deputy
Permanent Representative of Italy to the
United Nations

Moderator: **Prof. Urs Gauchat**, Dean of the College
of Architecture and Design, New Jersey
Institute of Technology (NJIT);
Consortium for Sustainable Urbanization

Panel:

Mr. Nicholas Hamilton, Director of Urban Policy,
The American Assembly

Mr. Floris Alkemade, Chief Government Architect,
the Netherlands

Hon. Jose Torres, Mayor of Paterson, New Jersey,
USA

Ms. Carol Loewenson, President of AIA NY Chapter,
Partner, Mitchell, Giurgola Architects

Mr. Vinícius Carvalho Pinheiro, Special
Representative to the UN and Director ILO Office for
the United Nations

Q&A and discussion

4.00 pm   **Dialogue Session II: Challenges and opportunities**

Moderator: **Mr. Frederic Vallier**, Secretary General
of the Council of European
Municipalities and Regions

Panel:

Mr. Don Weinreich and Ms. **Eliza Montgomery**, ENNEAD Lab (UNHCR-Stanford Project)

Mr. Filiep Decorte, Deputy Director, UN-Habitat New York Office

Hon. Lefteris Papagiannakis, Vice Mayor of Athens, Greece

Dr. Aliye Pekin Celik, President, Consortium for Sustainable Urbanization

Q&A and discussion

5.00 pm **Way forward**

Chair: **H.E. Dr. Nawaf Salam,** Permanent Representative of Lebanon to the United Nations

Moderator: **Prof. Lance Jay Brown**, ACSA Distinguished Professor of Architecture, Bernard and Anne Spitzer School of Architecture, City College of New York; Consortium for Sustainable Urbanization

Panel:

Hon. Berry Vrbanovic, Mayor of Kitchener, Canada

Dr. Lucy Earle, Urban Advisor, International Rescue Committee

Ms. Ninette Kelley, Director, New York Office, United Nations High Commissioner for Refugees

Ms. Michele Klein-Solomon, Director of the Secretariat of Migrants in Countries in Crisis International Organization for Migration

Mr. Fabrizio Hochschild, Deputy to the SG's Special Advisor for the Summit on Addressing Large Movements of Refugees and Migrants

Q&A and discussion

5.45 pm   Concluding remarks

Ms. Emilia Saiz, Deputy Secretary General, United
Cities and Local Governments

Mr. James Mc Cullar, FAIA, VP Consortium for
Sustainable Urbanization, Past President, AIANY
Chapter

Ms. Yamina Djacta, Director, UN-Habitat New York Office

ANNEX 4: MEETING ORGANIZERS

 The Consortium for Sustainable Urbanization is a New York based, non-for-profit organization 501(c)(3) formed to promote a better understanding of the role of sustainable urbanization and resilient design in the planning of our cities with a newfound optimism about the urban future.

Our purpose is to advocate for responsible and enlightened planning and design. We believe that a cross-sectoral approach can reduce the negative impact of mass migration to cities and improve the quality of life for all. We are committed to make urbanization sustainable.

We connect the global thought leaders concerned with urbanization in order to exchange ideas in high-level meetings and public forums. We disseminate information on-line, in print and in conferences. Our focus is on replicable ideas and concepts, best practices and speculative proposals.

Board Members

Lance Jay Brown, Founding Member
Aliye P. Çelik, Founding Member and President
Ludivine Cornille, Director of Programs
Urs Gauchat, Founding Member
Theodore Liebman
James McCullar, Founding Member and Vice-President
H. Öner Yurtseven, Treasurer

Honorary Council Members

H.E. Dr. Talal Abu-Ghazaleh, Chairman,
Ana Marie Argilagos
Megan Sterling Chusid
Thomas Dallessio
Robert Geddes
Sarbuland Khan
Maxinne Leighton

Margaret O'Donoghue Castillo
Lisa Staiano-Coico
Theresa Williamson
Erich Winkler
Tom Wright

Fellows: Antonieta Castro-Cosio, Florian Lux, Amanda Prins, and
Ashley Simone

Interns: Irem Ayan, Inna Branzburg, Marilyn Cheong, Courtney
Prince, and Alex Spatz

Talal Abu-Ghazaleh Organization

The Talal Abu-Ghazaleh Organization (TAG) is the world's largest global group of professional service firms with expertise that spans a plethora of areas such as corporate governance, educational consultancy, economic and strategic studies, accounting external and internal audits, human resources, management advisory services, and more. TAG has 85 offices across the world that aim to provide a wide range of high quality international professional and educational services, and ultimately contribute to economic, social, and cultural development. It achieves its objective by guiding and assisting agencies, international organizations, Pan-Arab governmental funding organizations, and other leading companies in their intricate business and management decisions.

UN⊕HABITAT
FOR A BETTER URBAN FUTURE

UN Habitat is the United Nations program working towards a better urban future. Its mission is to promote socially and environmentally sustainable human settlements development and the achievement of adequate shelter for all. UN Habitat manages its work through its headquarters in Nairobi, Kenya; offices in New York, USA; and Cairo, Egypt, Rio de Janeiro, Brazil; Fukuoka, Japan.

United Cities and Local Governments is the largest local government organization in the world and advocates for democratic and innovative cooperation between local governments within the international community, standing as a voice promoting their values and objectives.

The American Institute of Architects

Founded in 1857, **the AIA New York Chapter** is the oldest and largest chapter of the American Institute of Architects. The Chapter's members include more than 5,000 practicing architects, allied professionals, students, and public members interested in architecture and design. The AIA New York Chapter is dedicated to three goals: design excellence, public outreach, and professional development.

The AIANY Design for Risk and Reconstruction Committee

The Design for Risk and Reconstruction Committee, DfRR, is set up to explore and address the potential for the design community to mitigate and adapt to disasters through the built environment. The mission of the committee is to foster awareness within the profession and the public of the necessity to anticipate risk from the scale of a building to comprehensive regional planning.

NETWORK

ELEVEN

DIGITAL TECHNOLOGIES
FOR SUSTAINABLE
URBANIZATION NETWORK

Network Eleven is an initiative by UN-Habitat and Talal Abu-Ghazaleh Organization

The Digital Technologies for Sustainable Urbanization Network (Network Eleven), co-chaired by Dr. Joan Clos, United Nations Under-Secretary-General and Executive Director of UN-Habitat, and Dr. Talal Abu-Ghazaleh, Chairman of the Talal Abu-Ghazaleh Organization (TAG-Org), aims to promote sharing of experiences and good practices in the use of digital technologies to deliver sustainable urbanization, and to contribute to the discussion towards the United Nations Conference on Housing and Sustainable Urban Development (Habitat3) and the New Urban Agenda, as well as the digital and urban dimensions of the 2030 Agenda for Sustainable Development. The launch of Network Eleven took place in 2015 in Barcelona, Spain The network will support implementation of the Sustainable Development Goal 11 (SDG 11) to "make cities and human settlements inclusive, save, resilient and sustainable."

Printed in Great Britain
by Amazon